ADULT COLORING BOOK

By The Beach

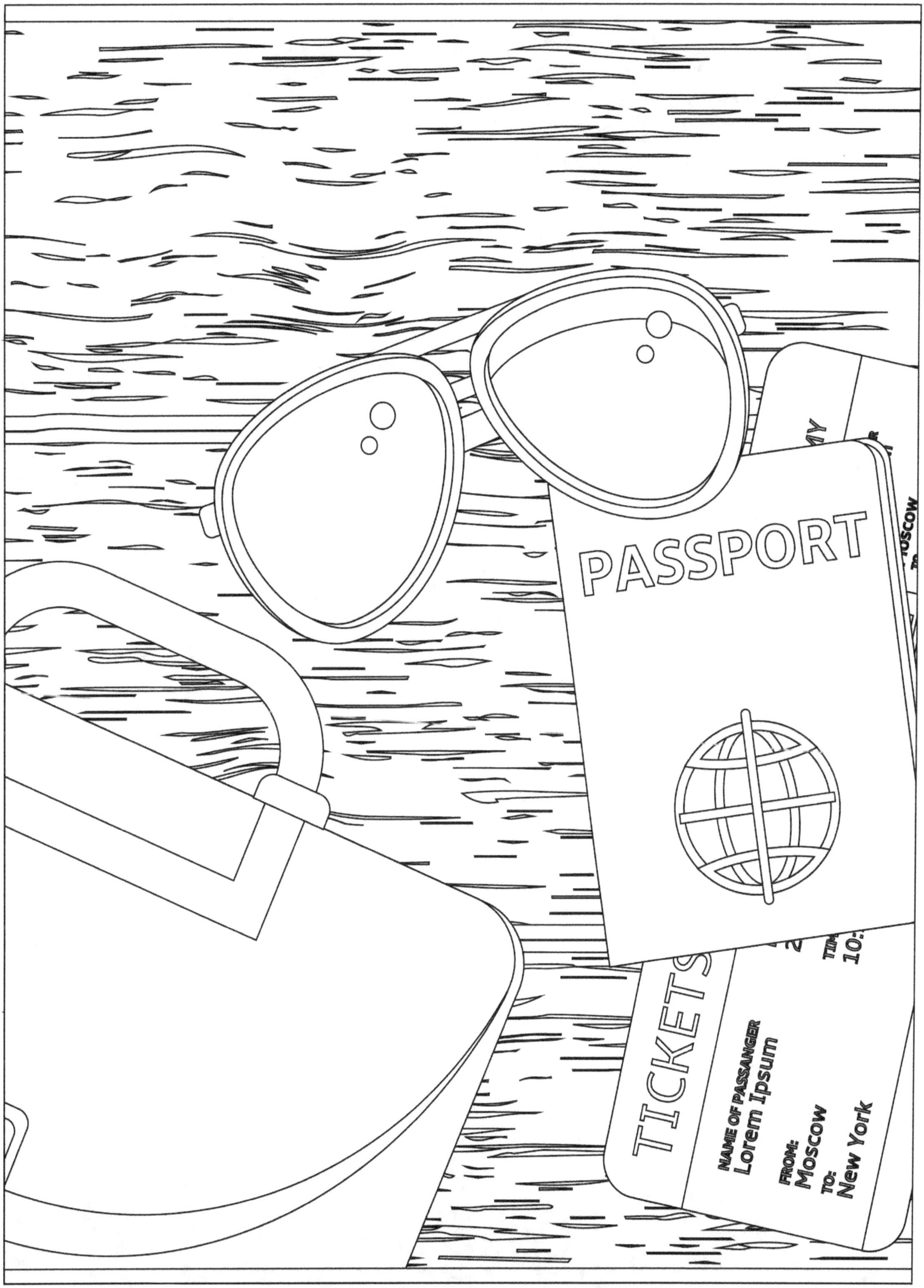
PASSPORT
TICKETS
NAME OF PASSANGER
Lorem Ipsum
FROM:
Moscow
TO:
New York

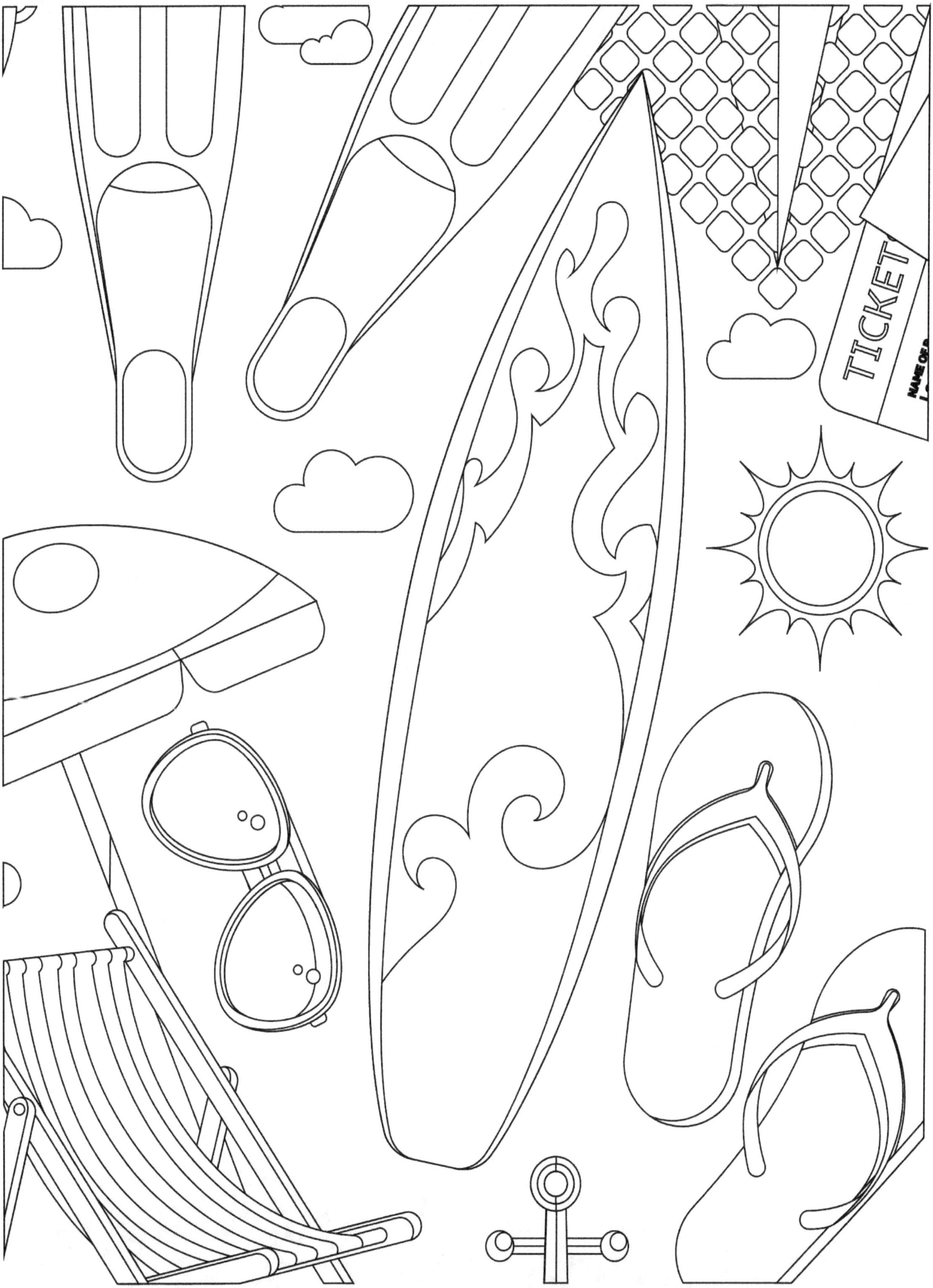
TICKET

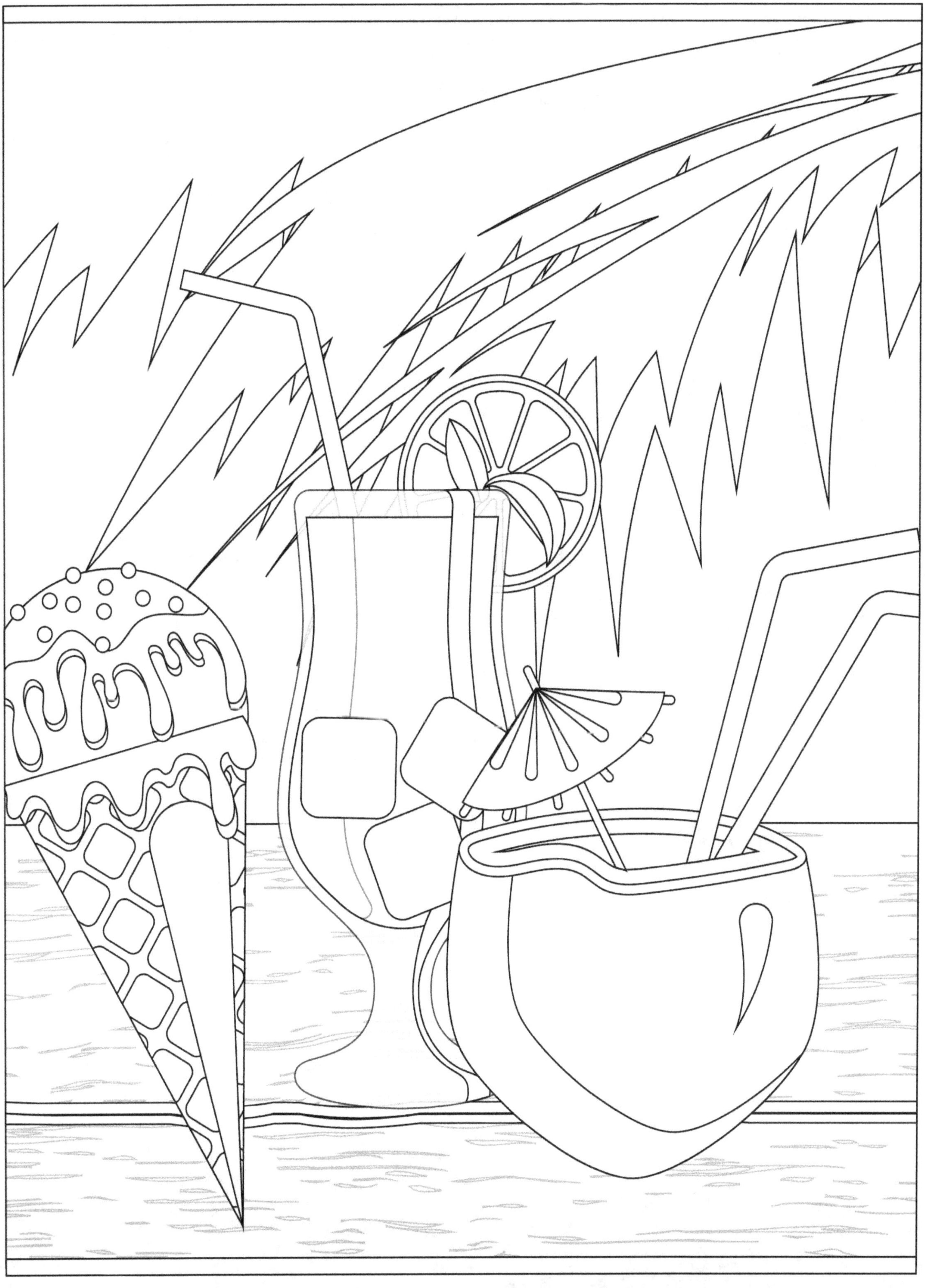

PASSPORT

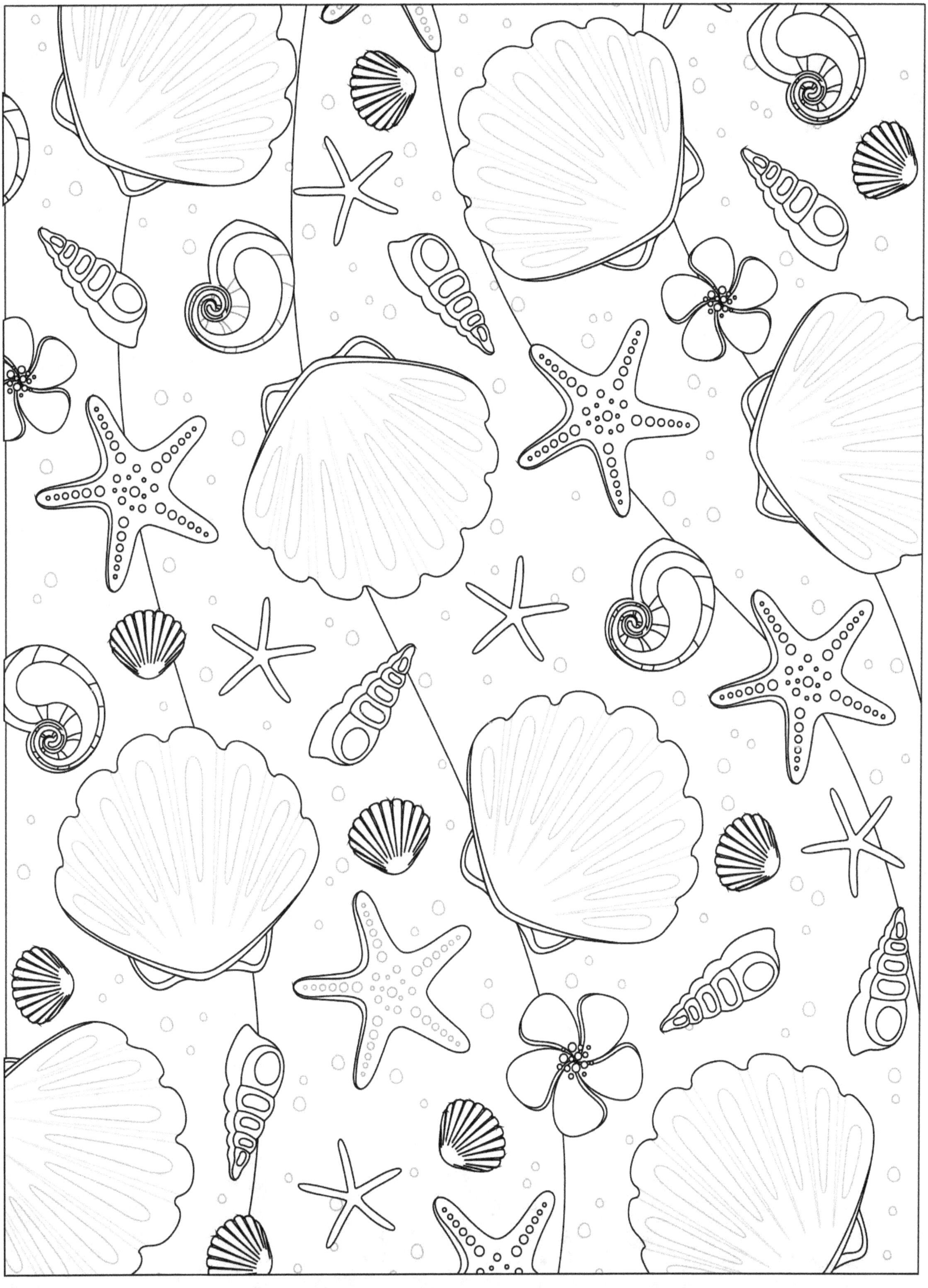

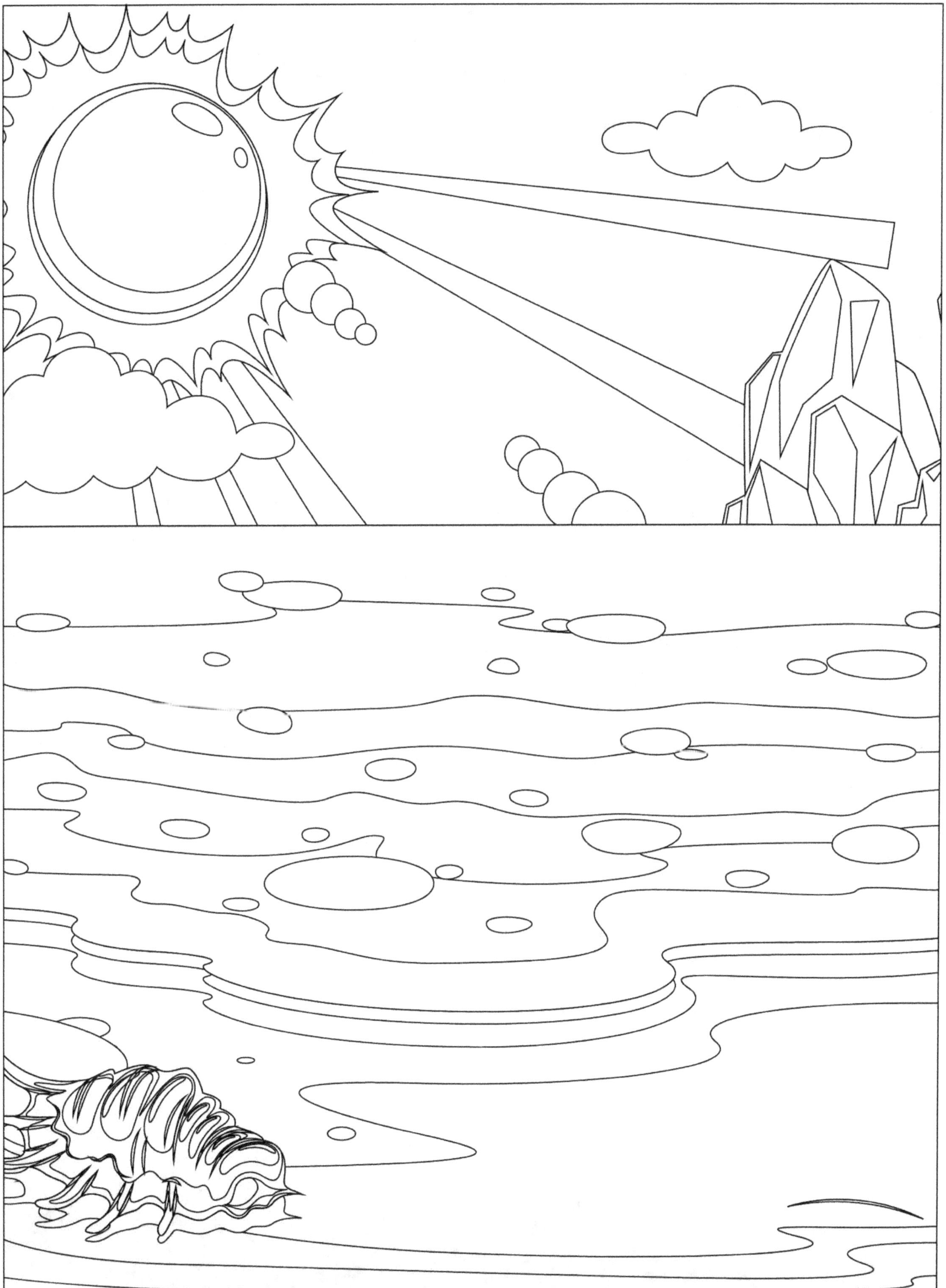

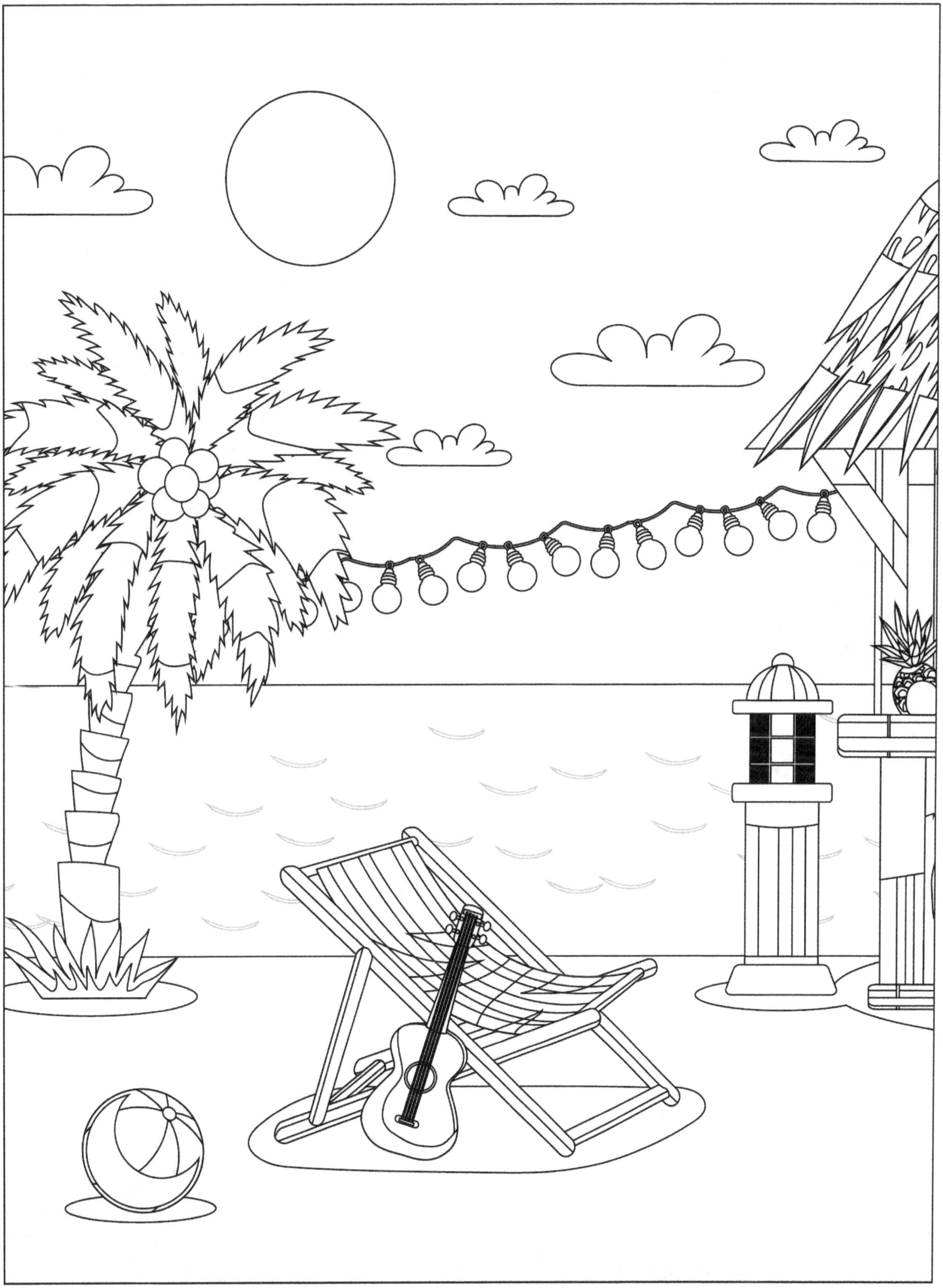

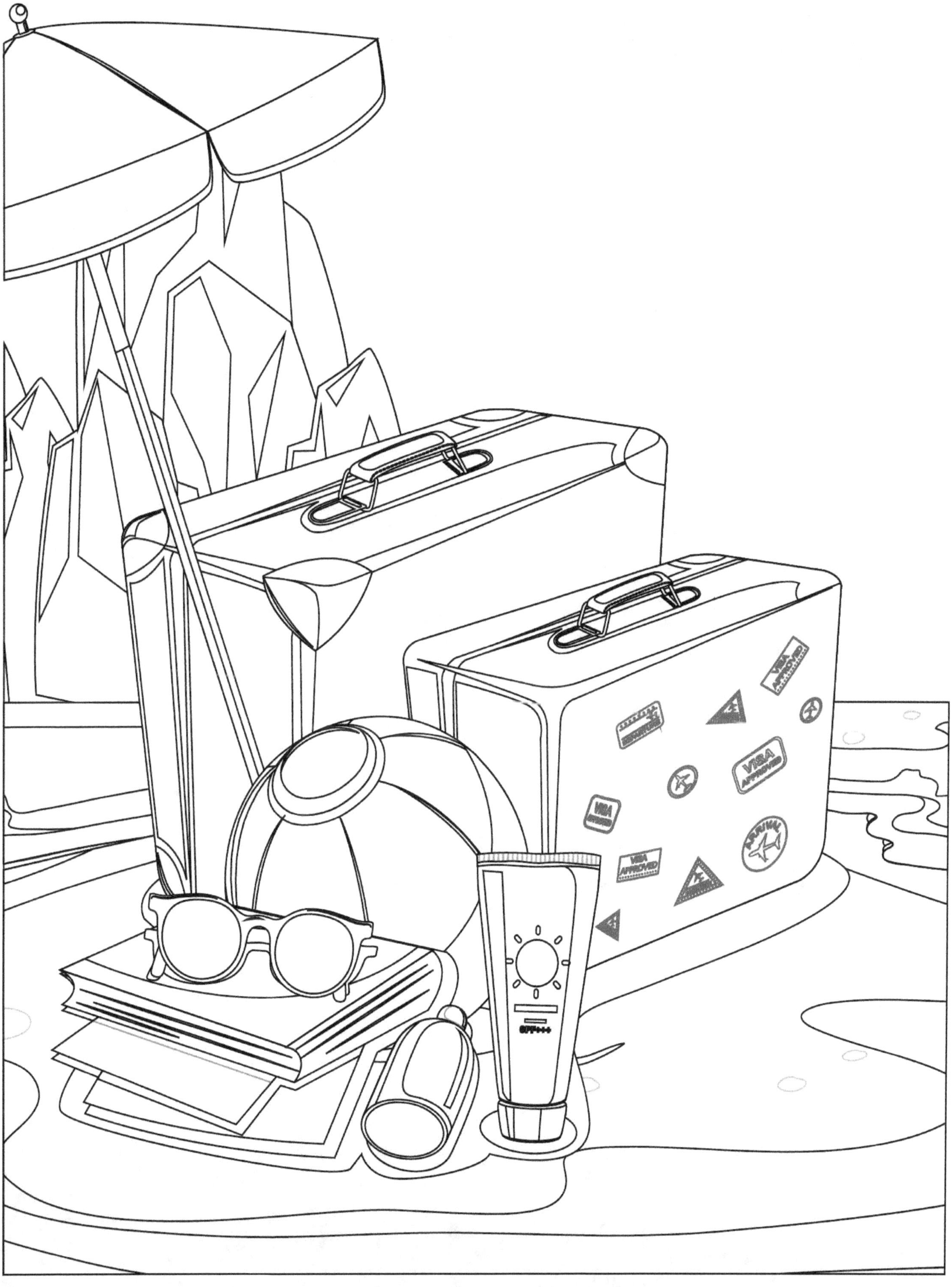
VISA APPROVED
VISA
VISA APPROVED

N
W
E
S
PASSPORT

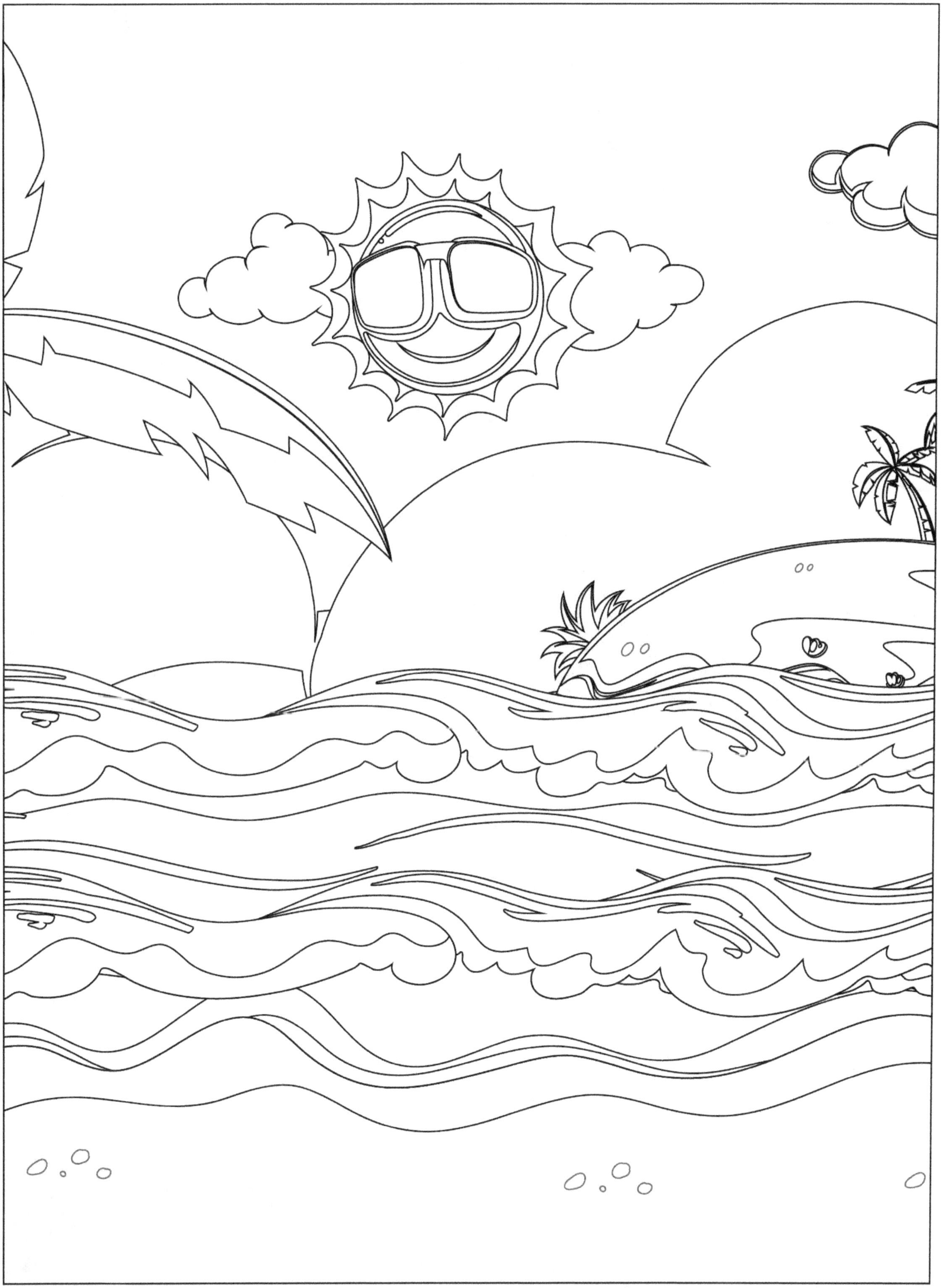

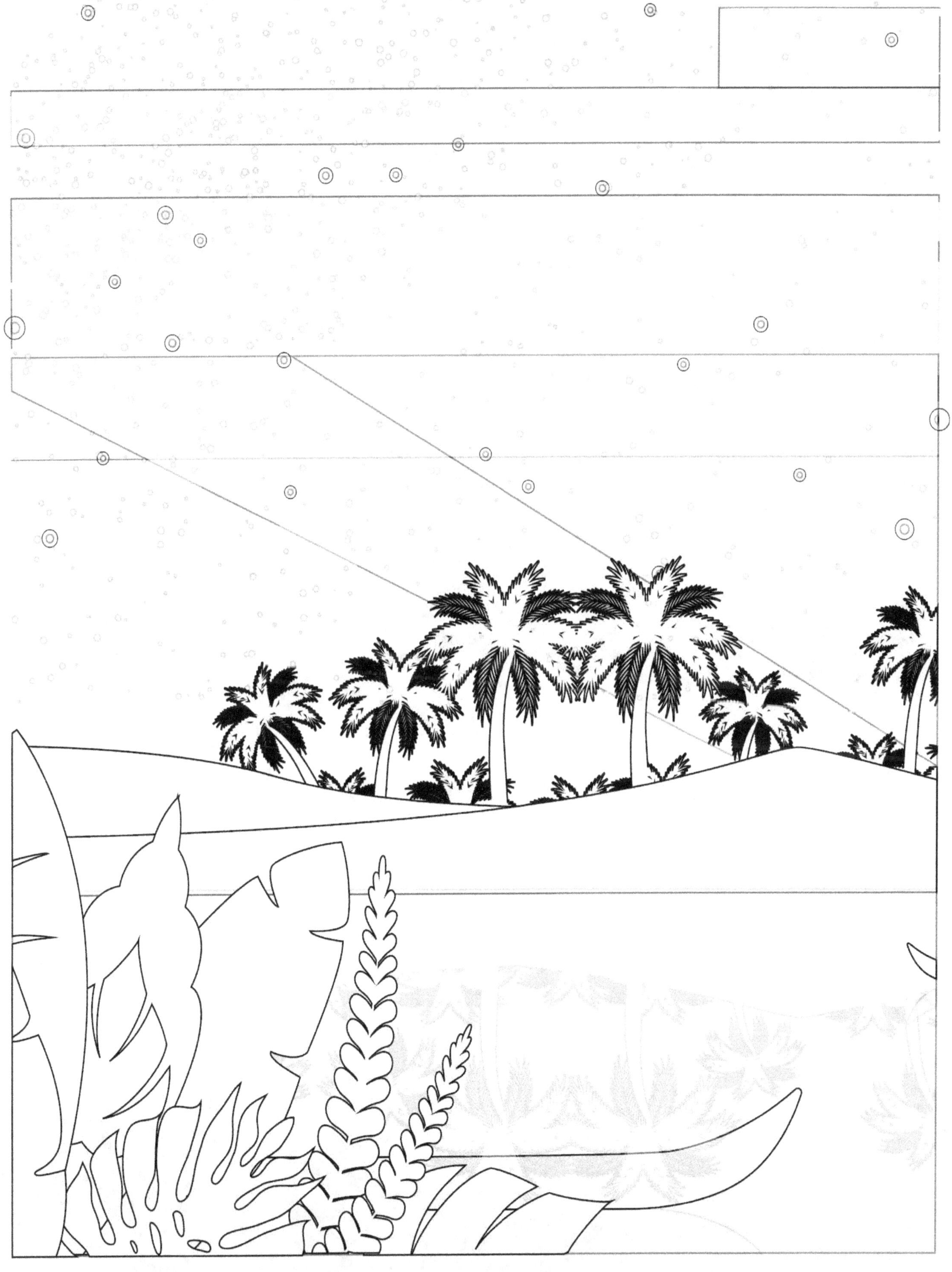

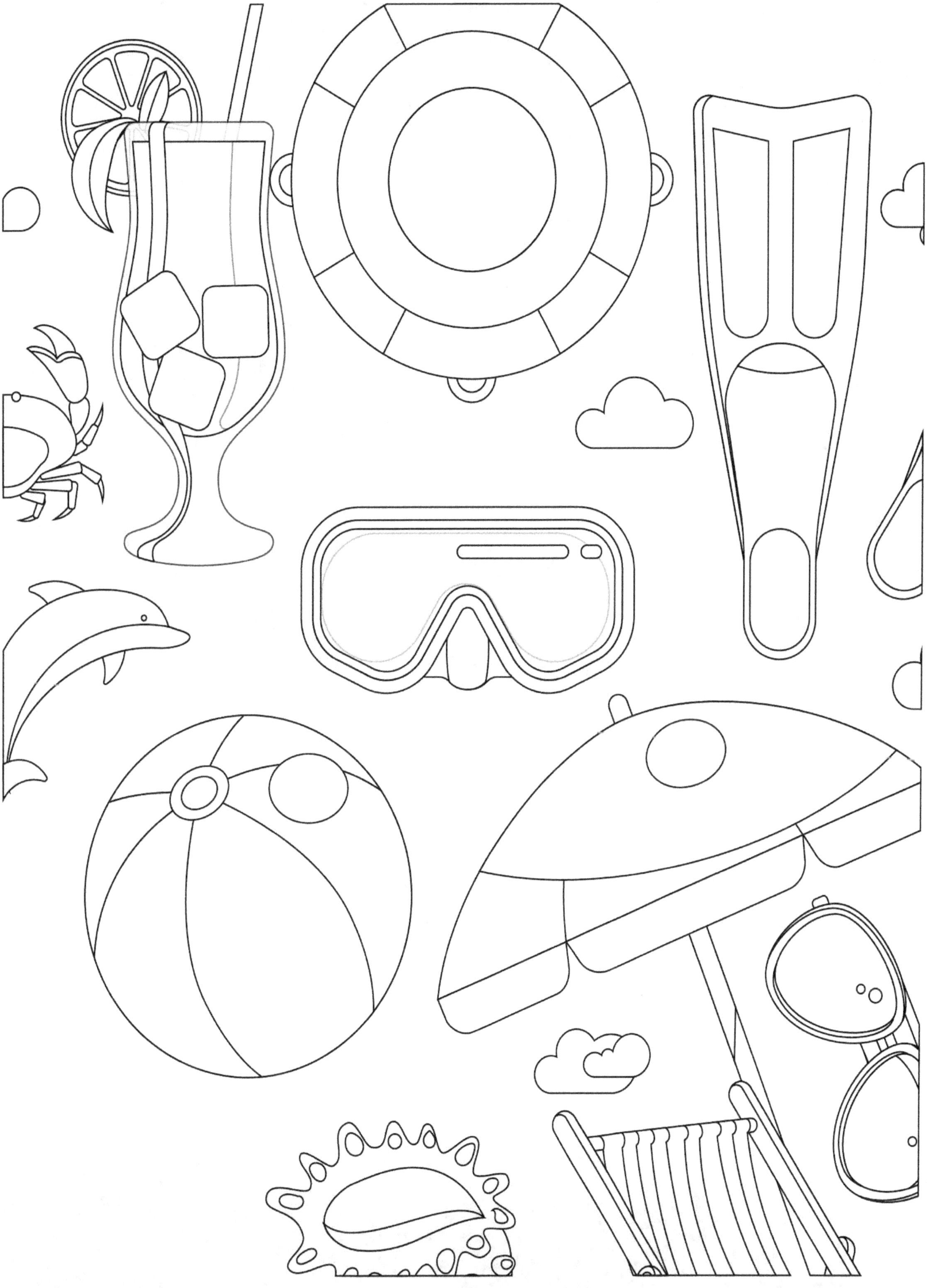

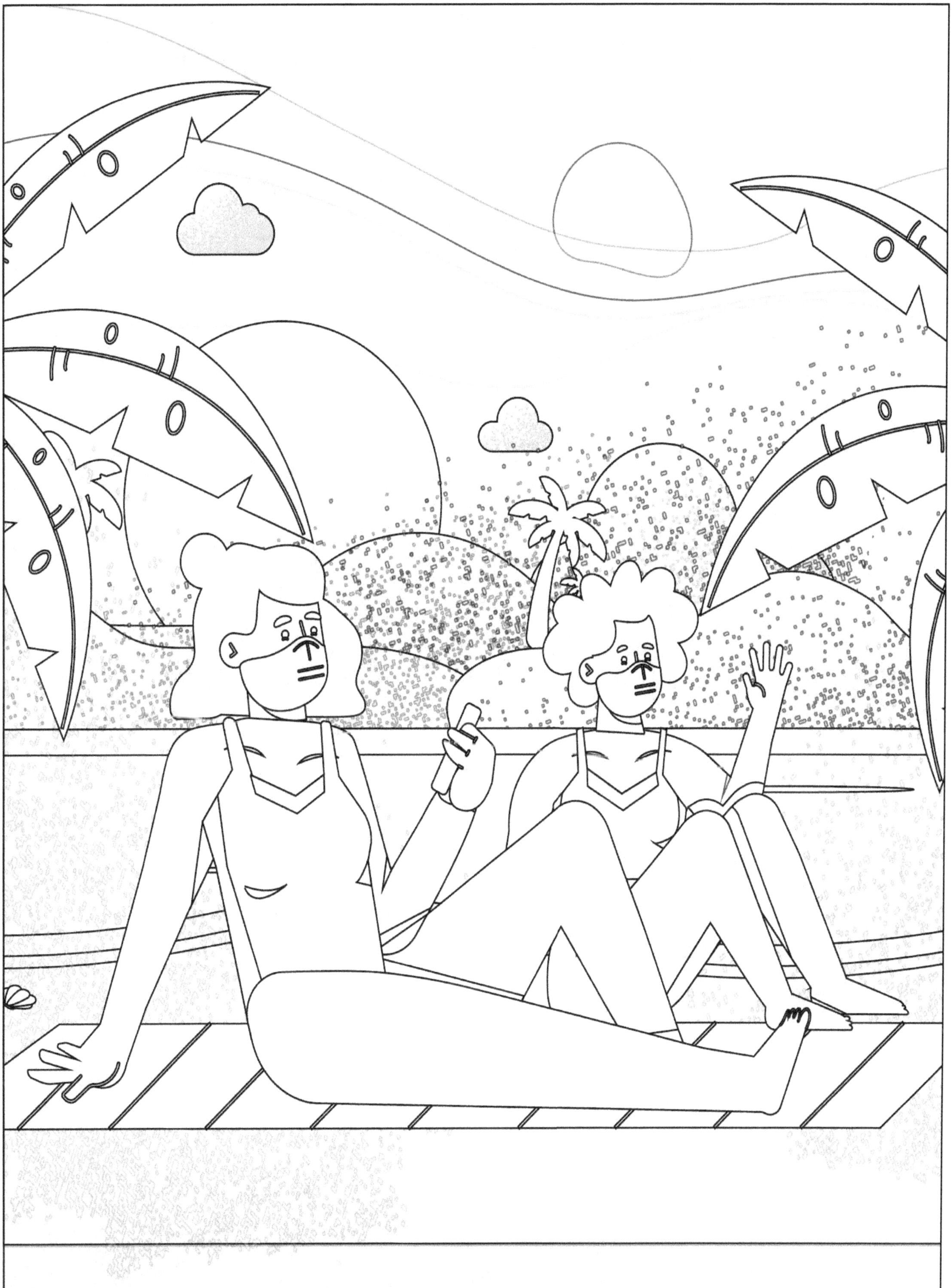

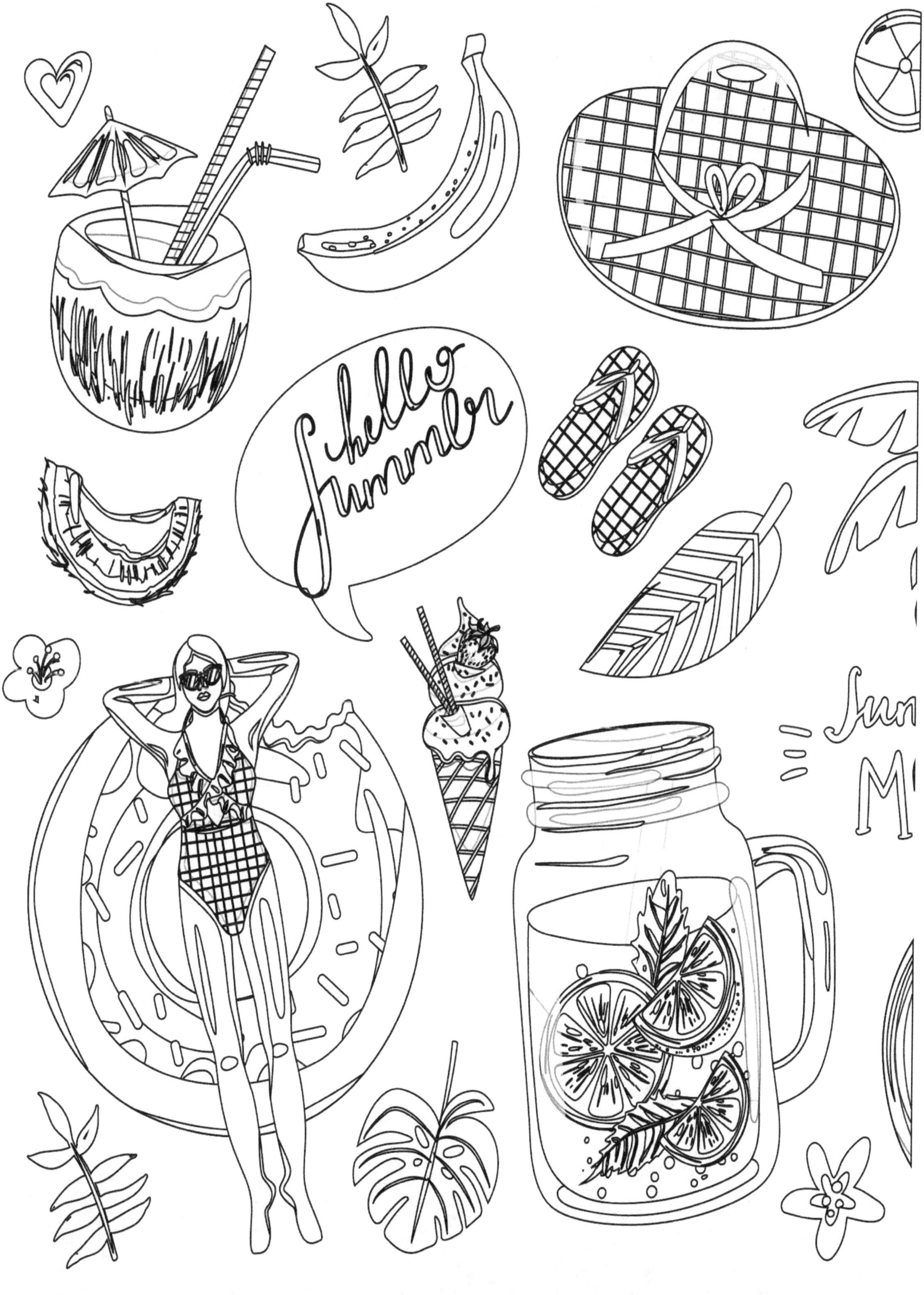
hello summer

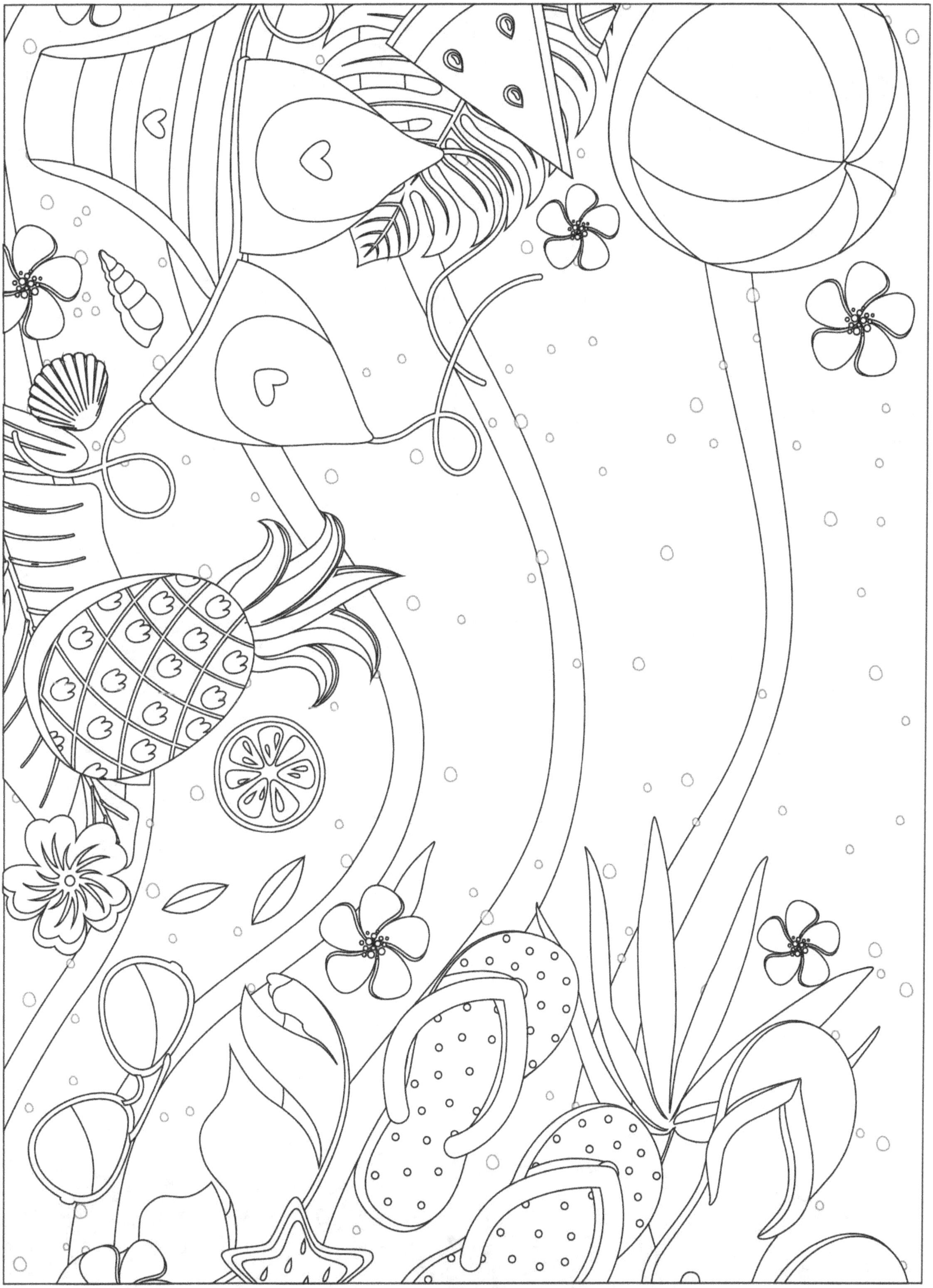

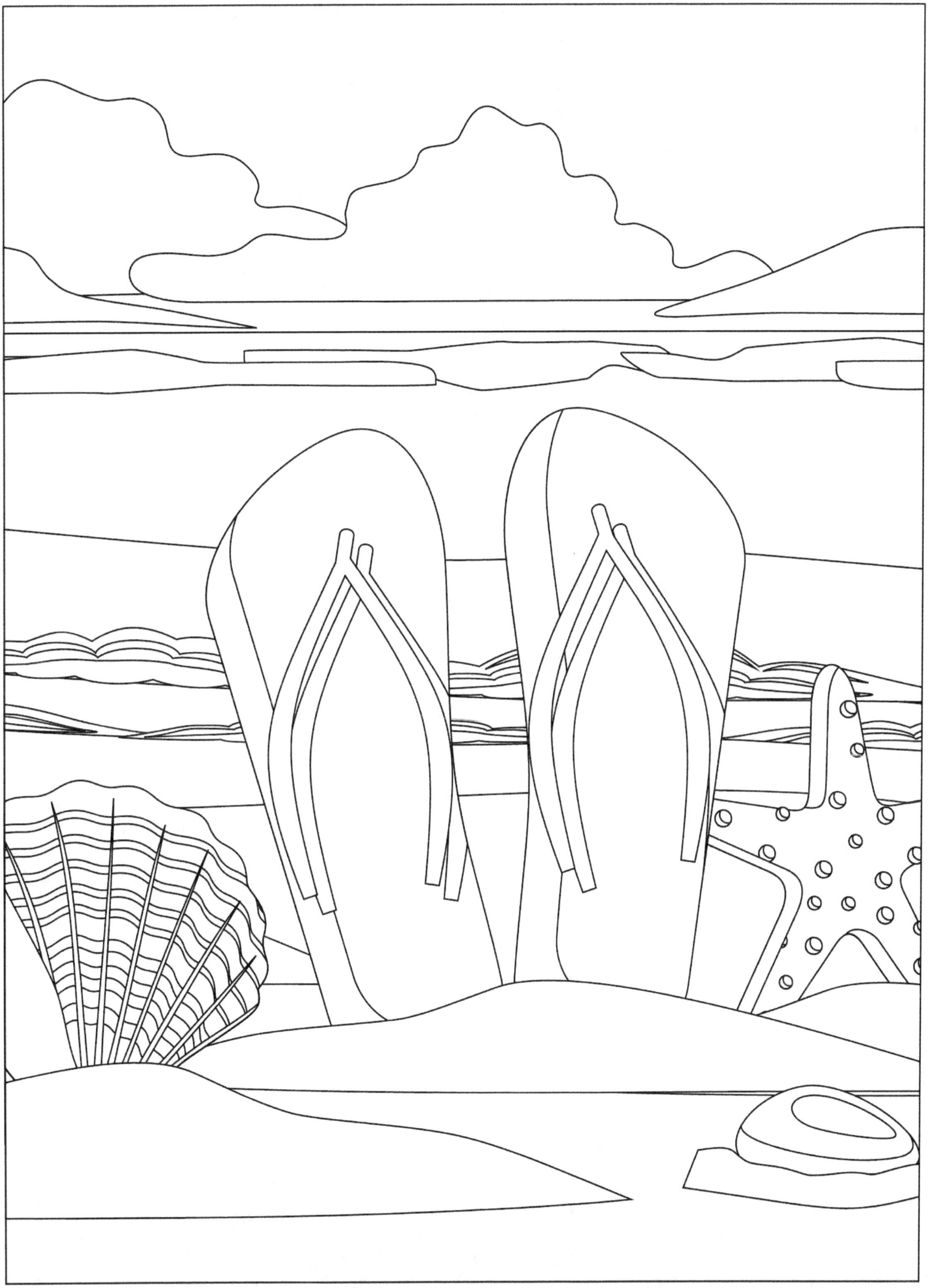

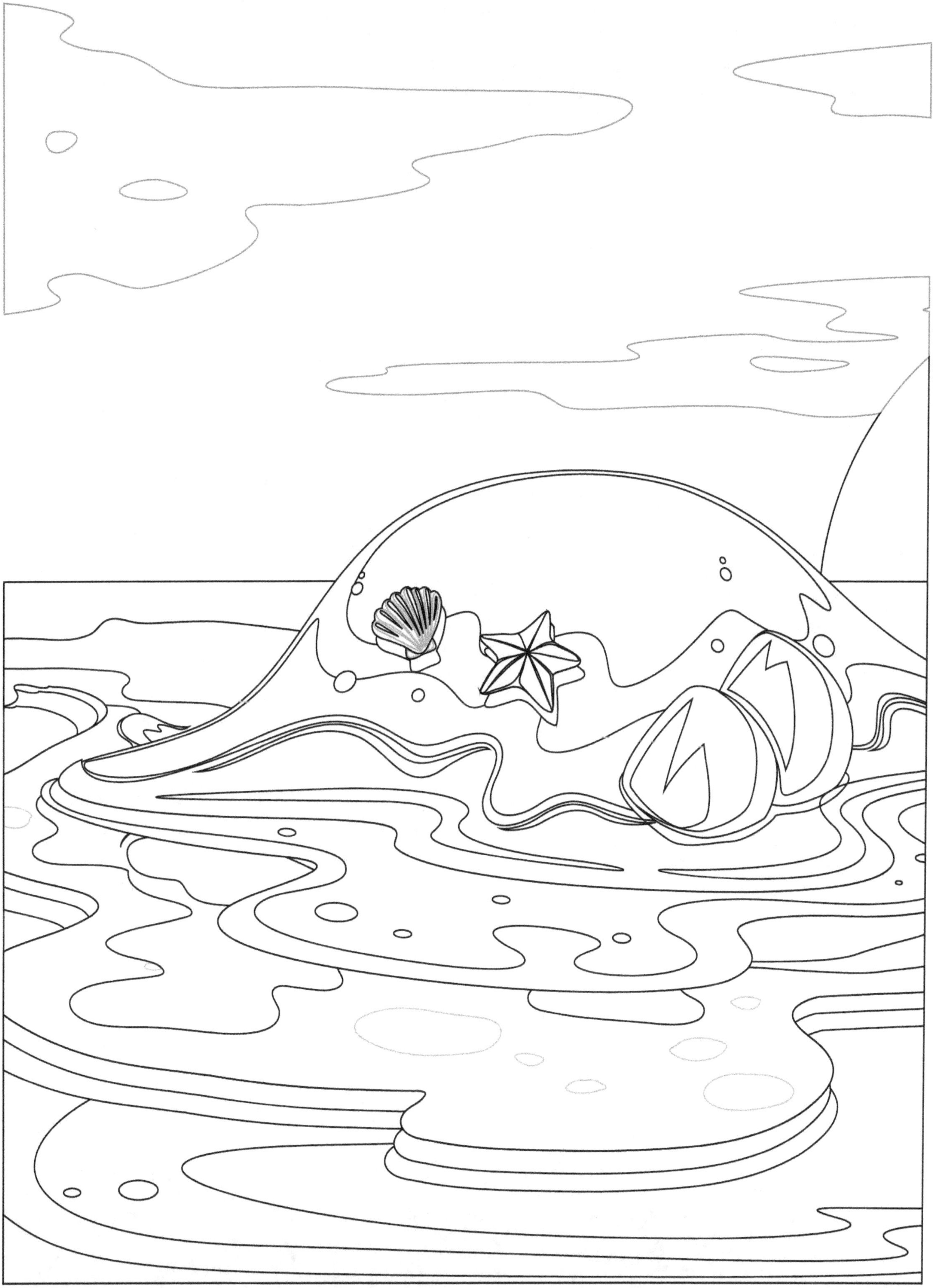

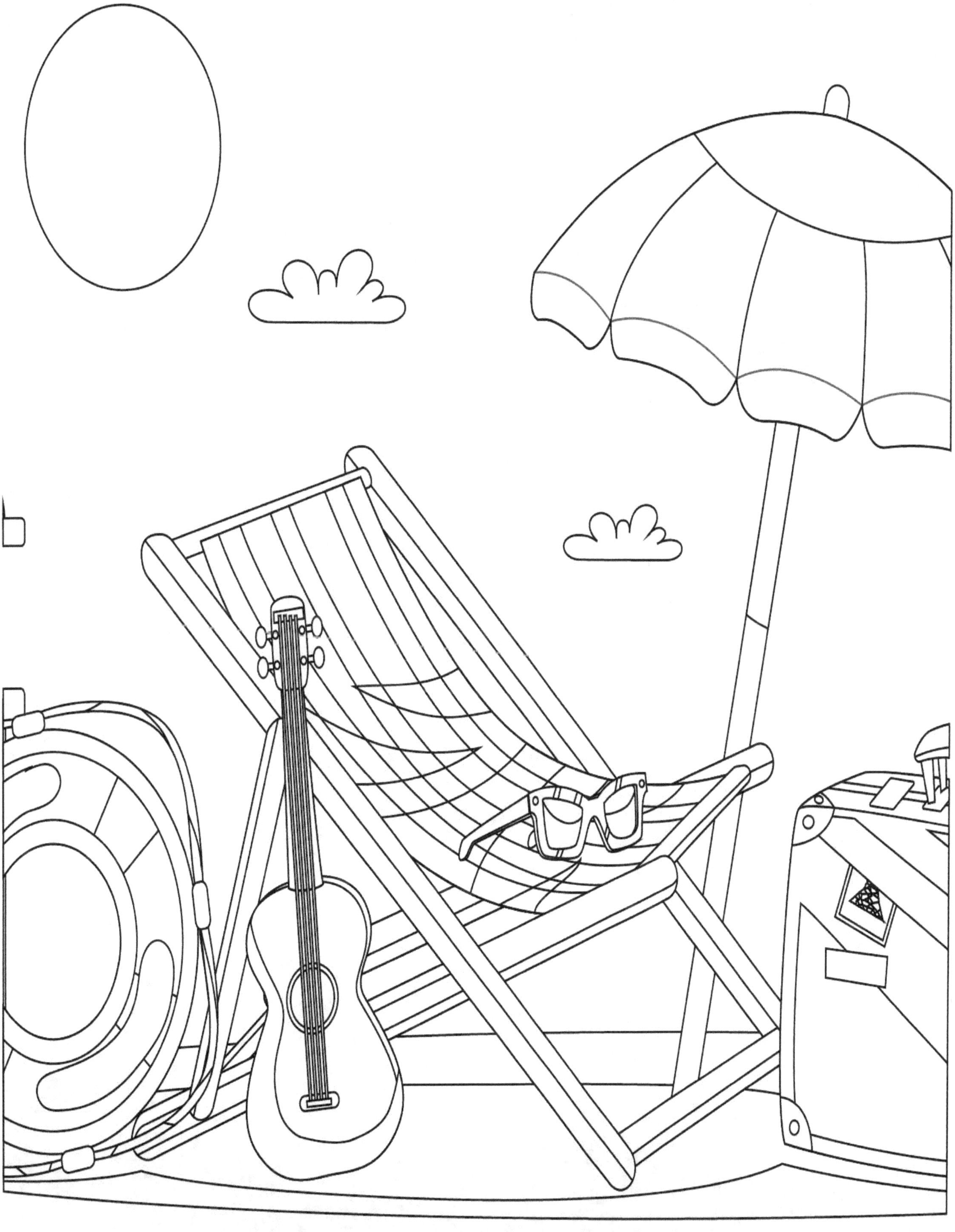

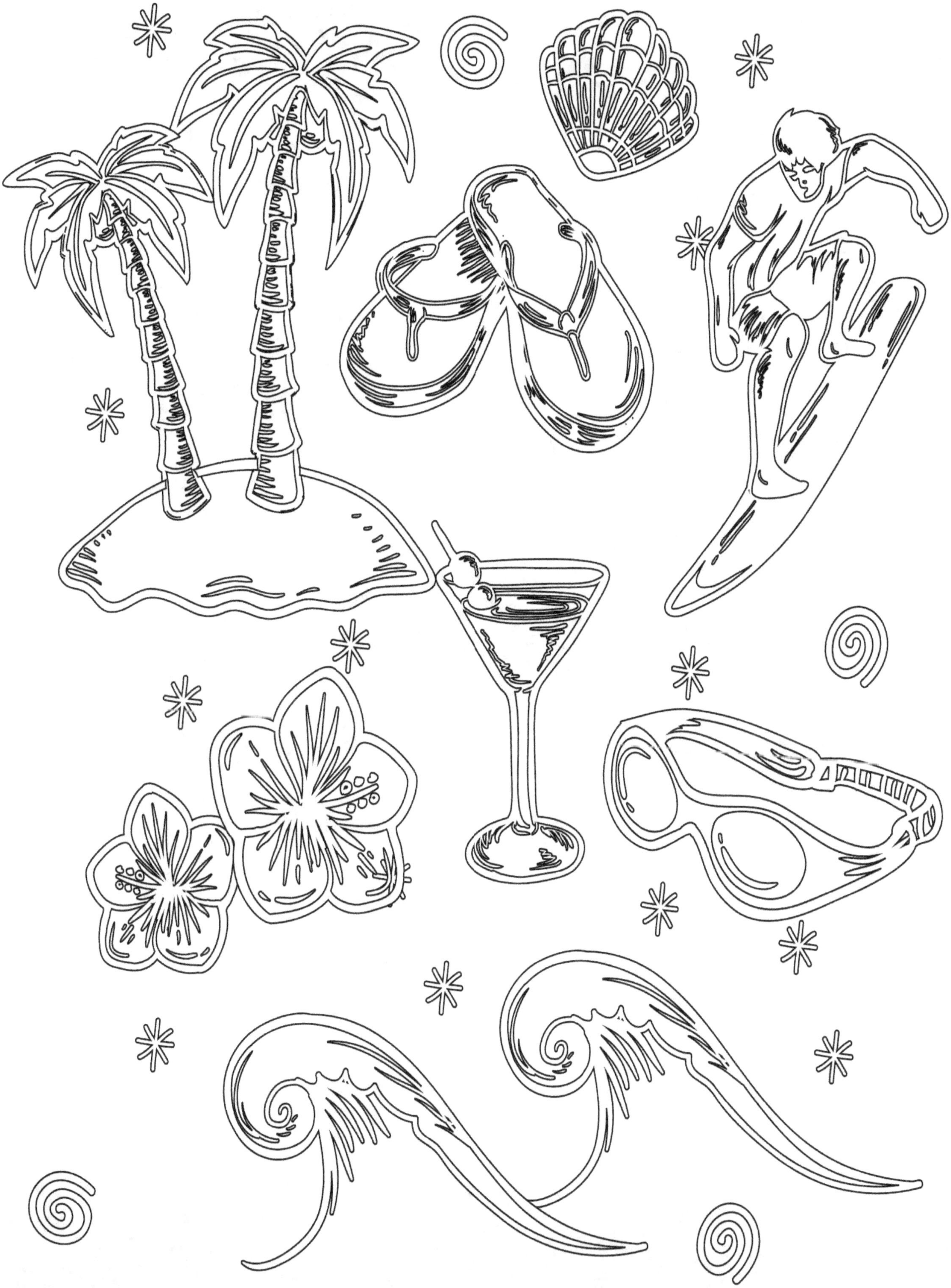

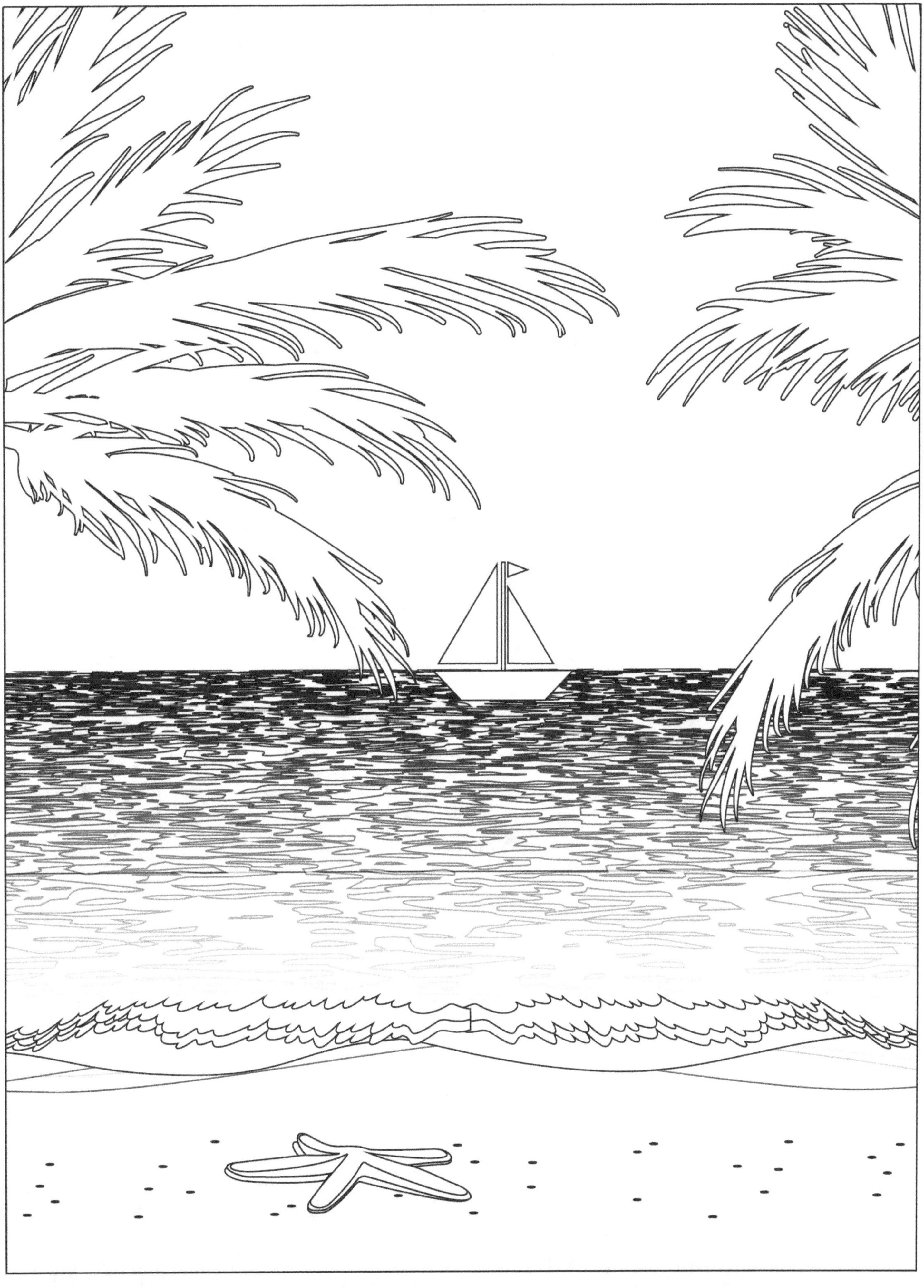

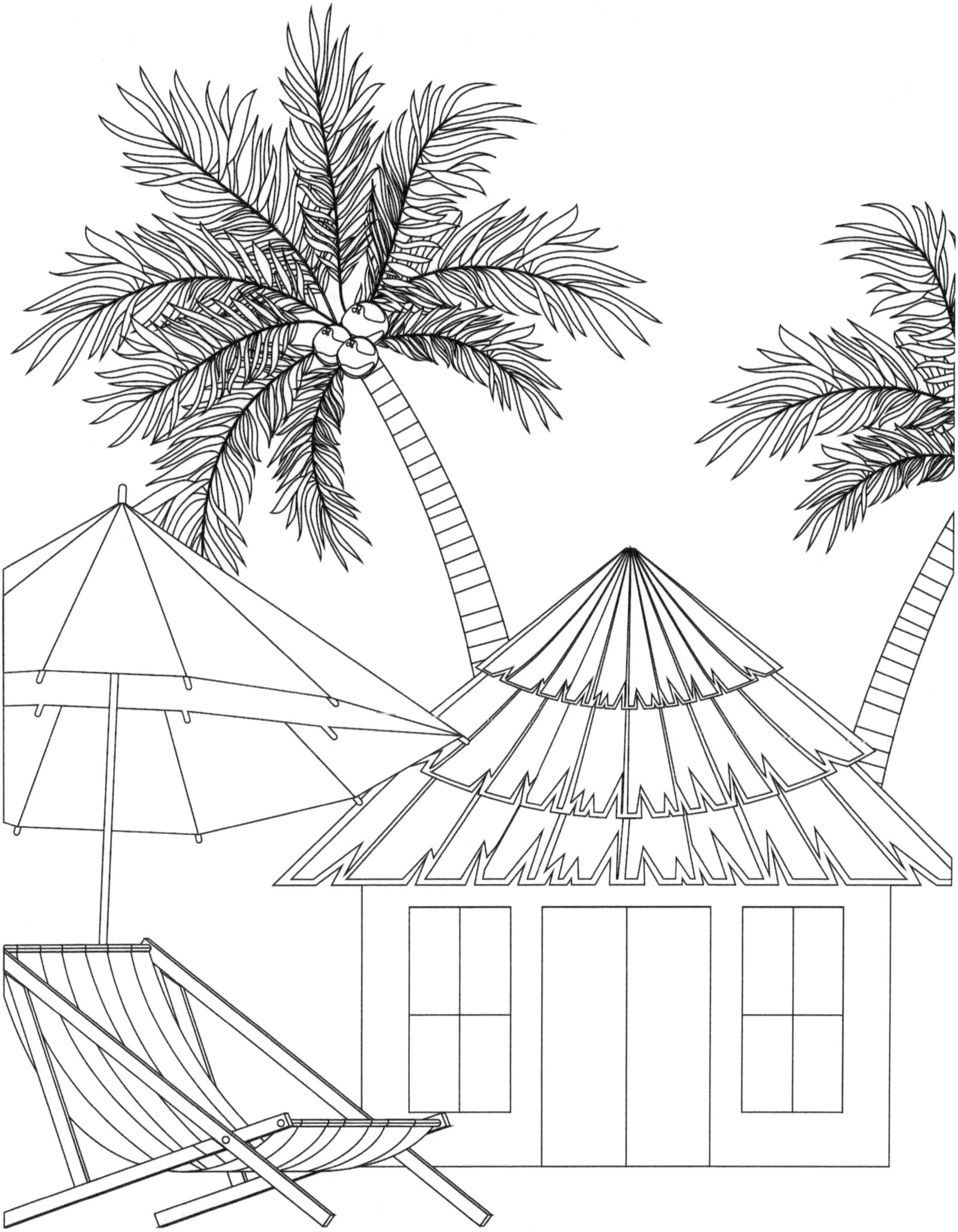

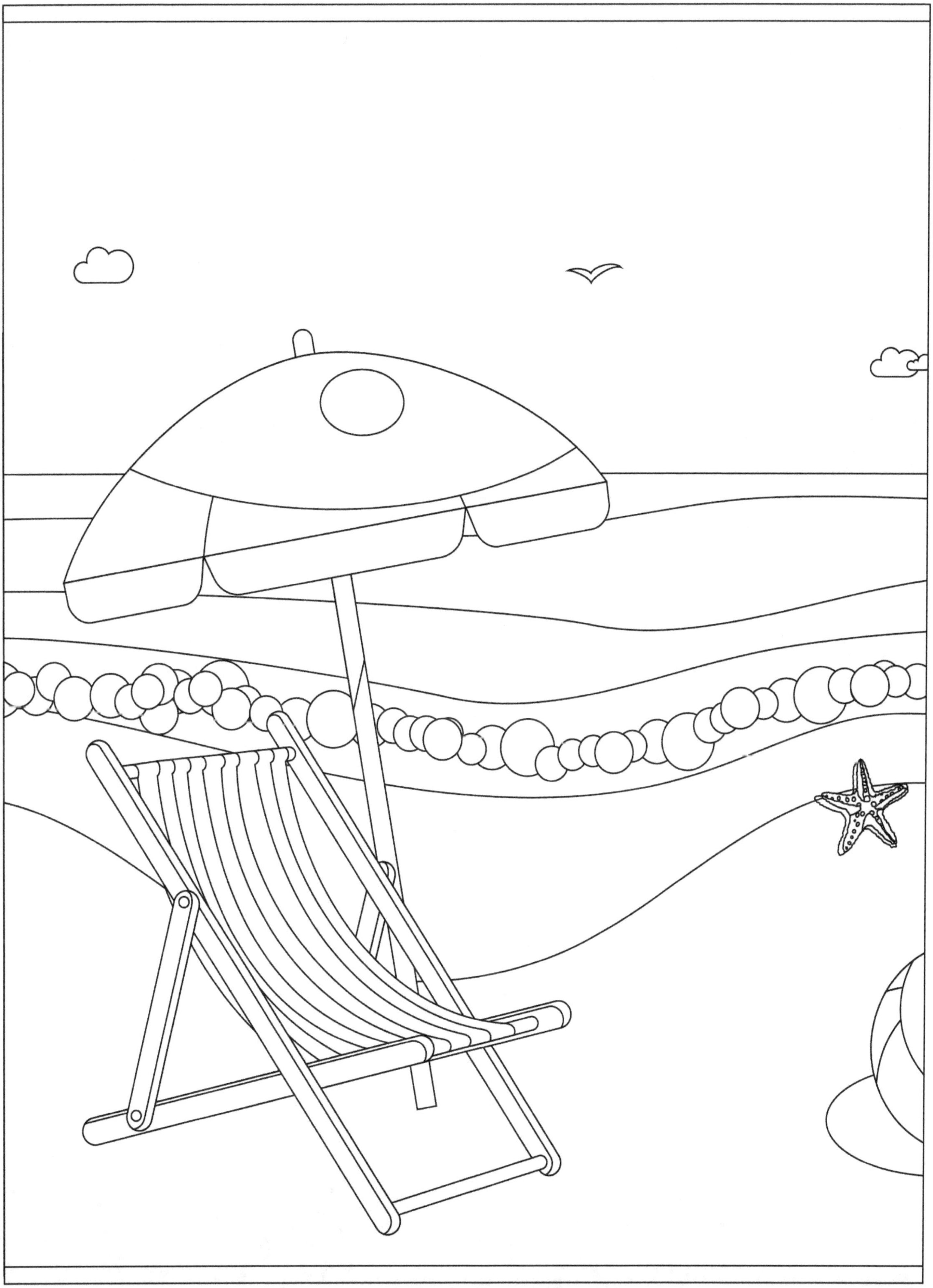

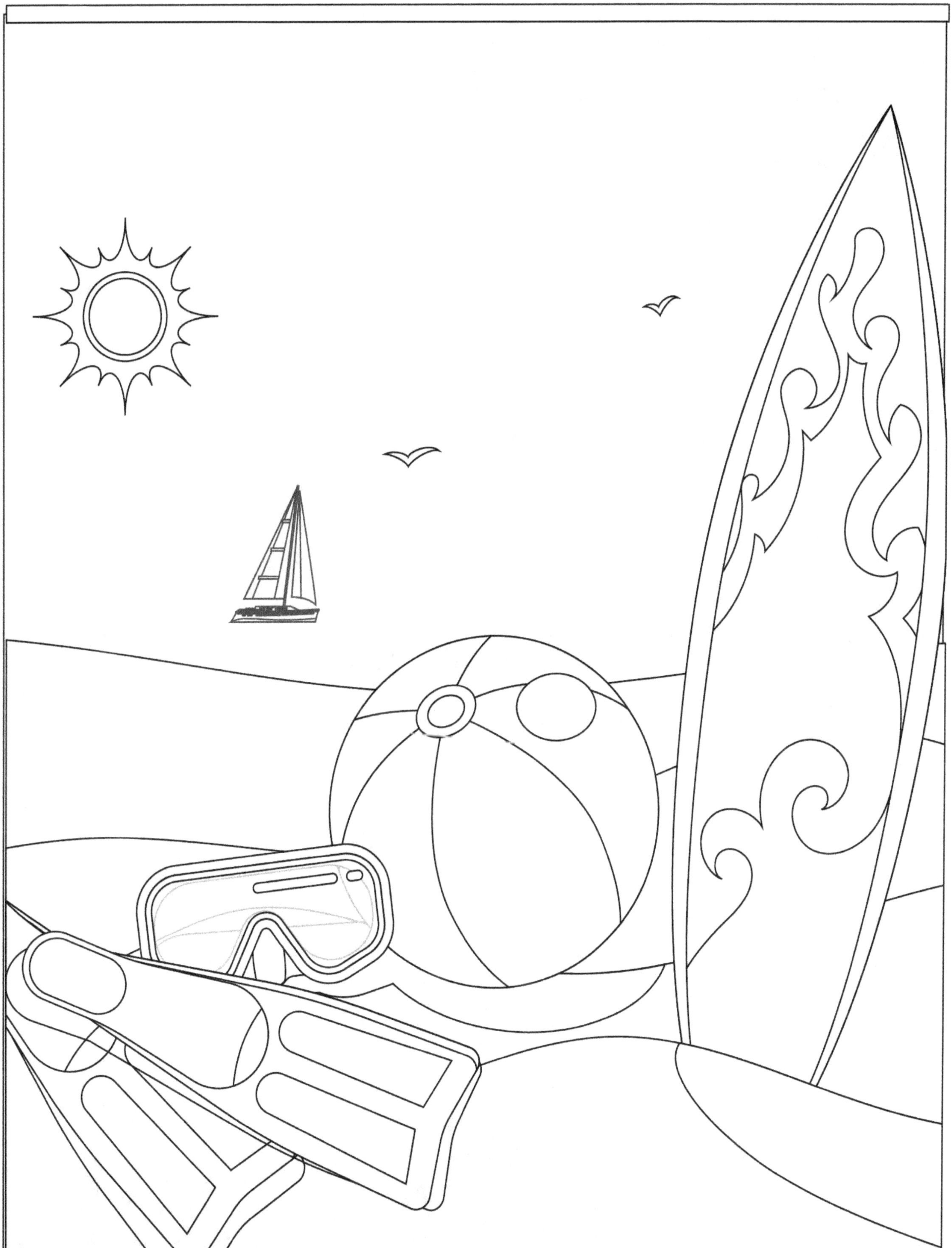

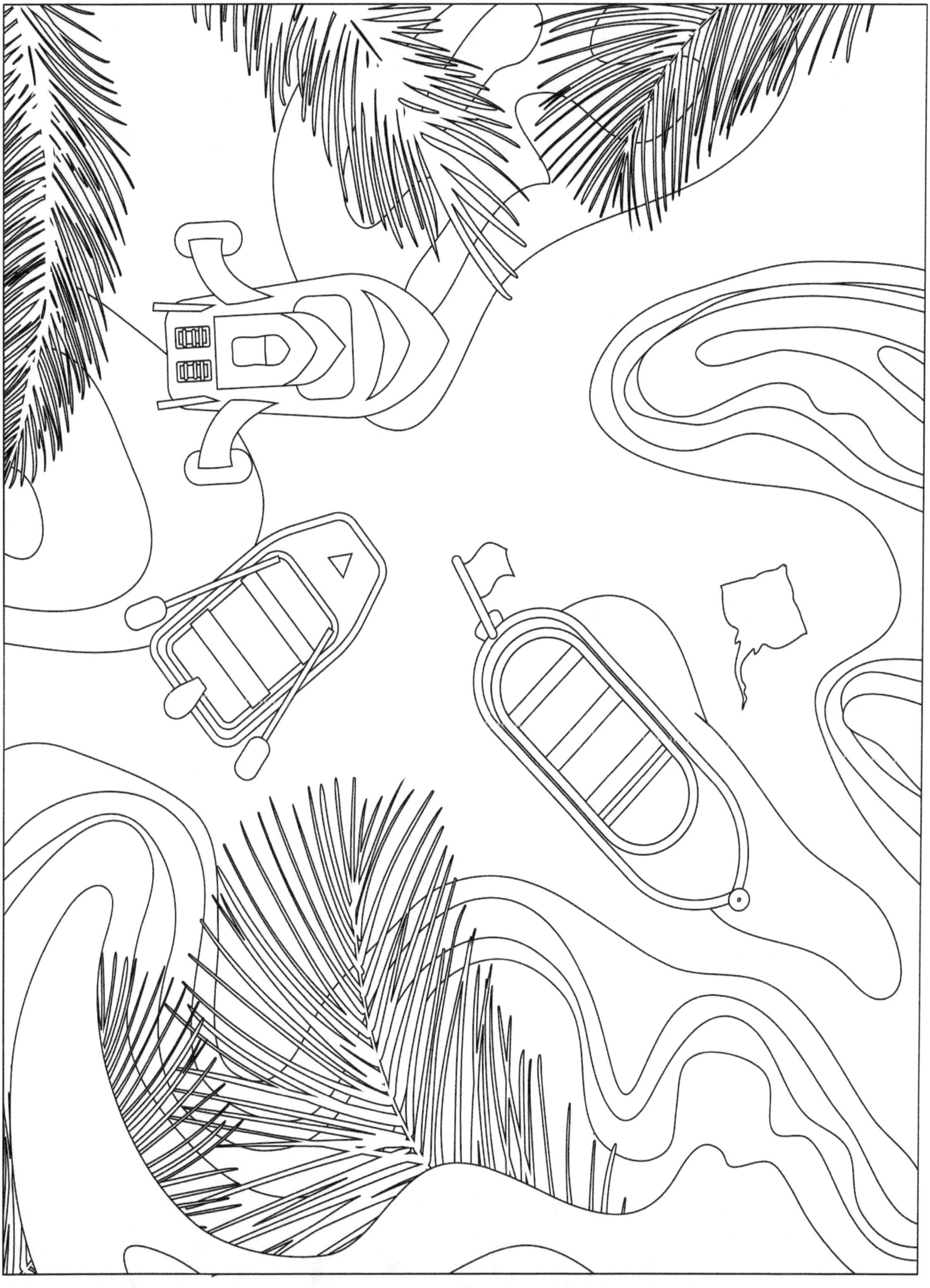

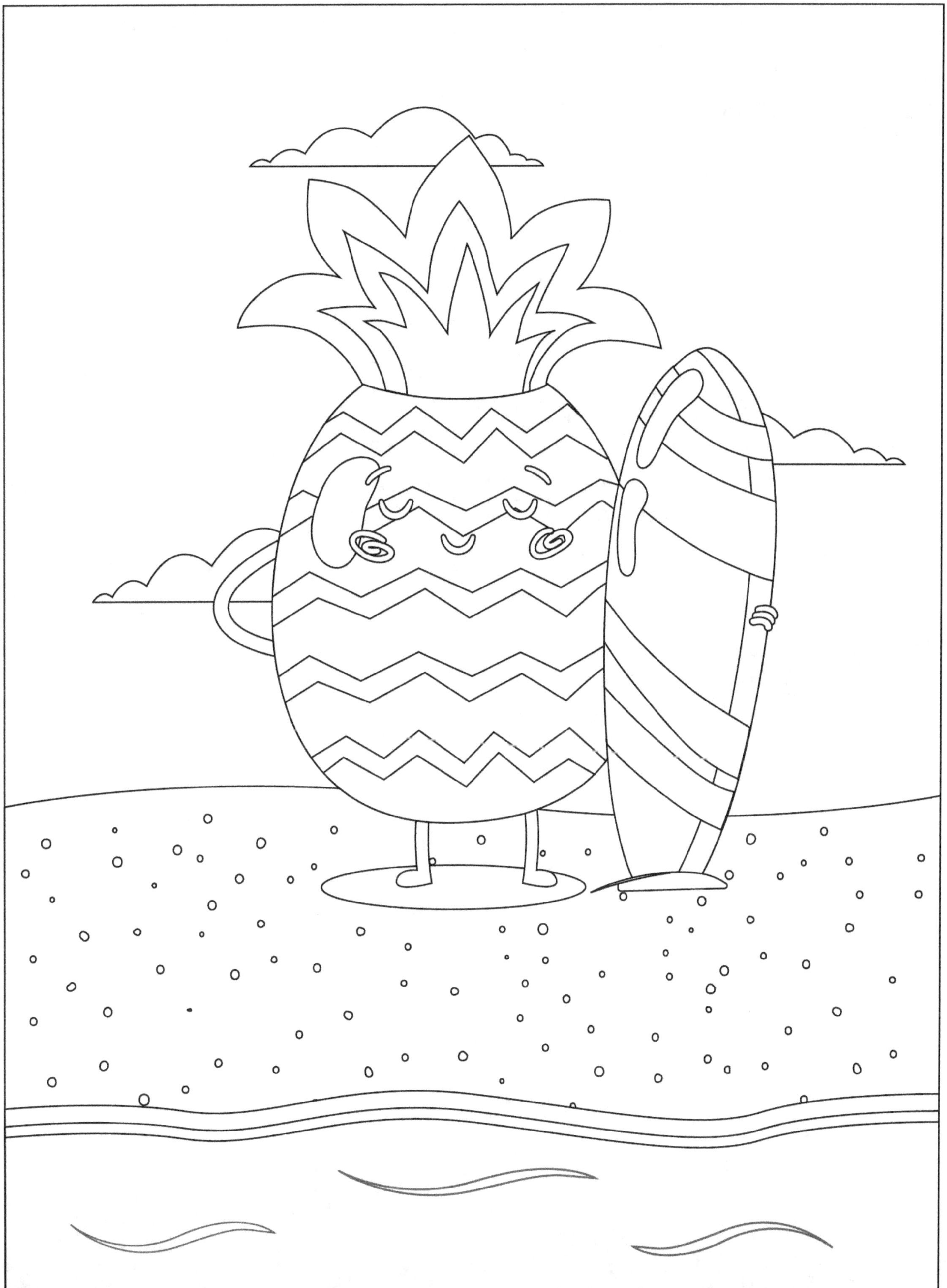

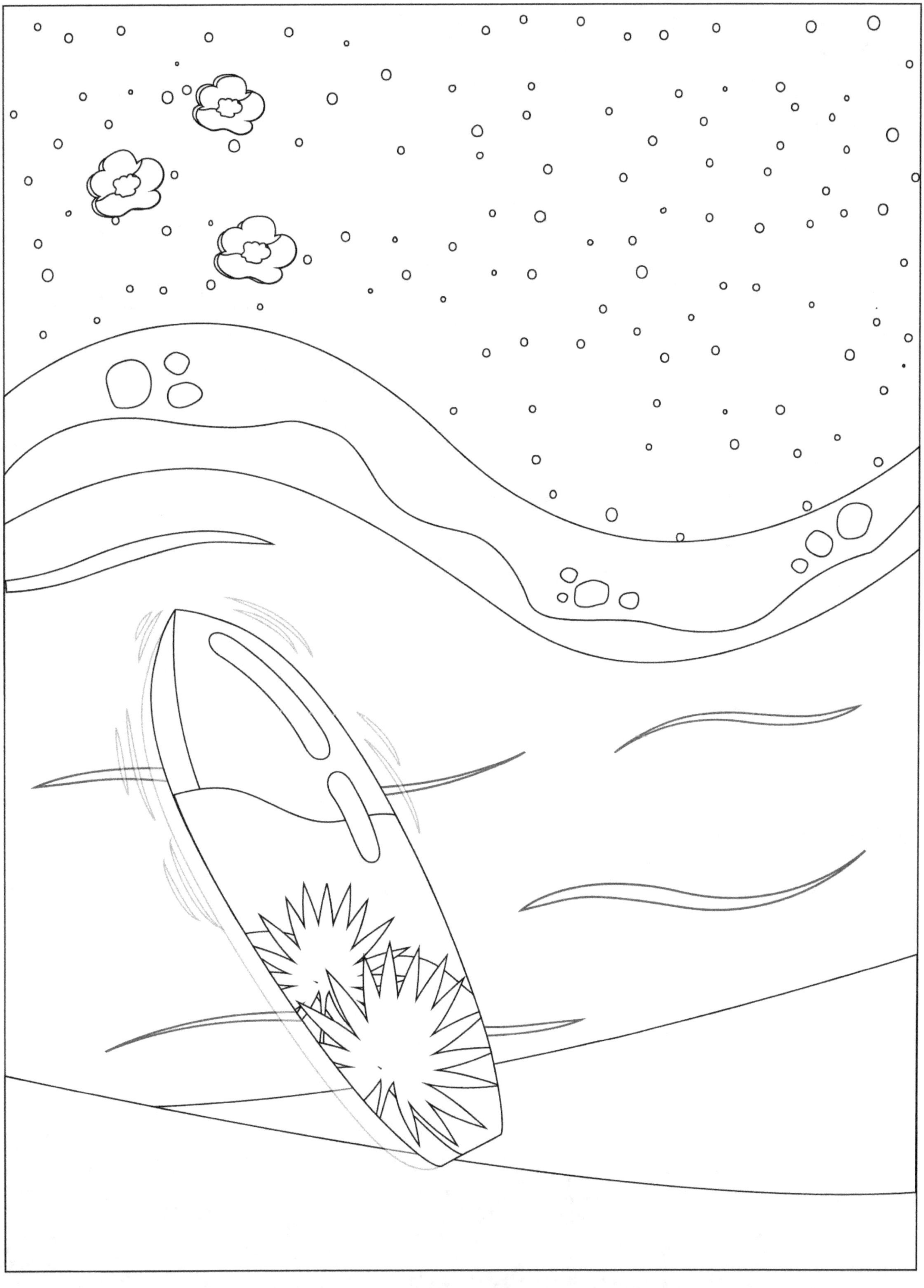

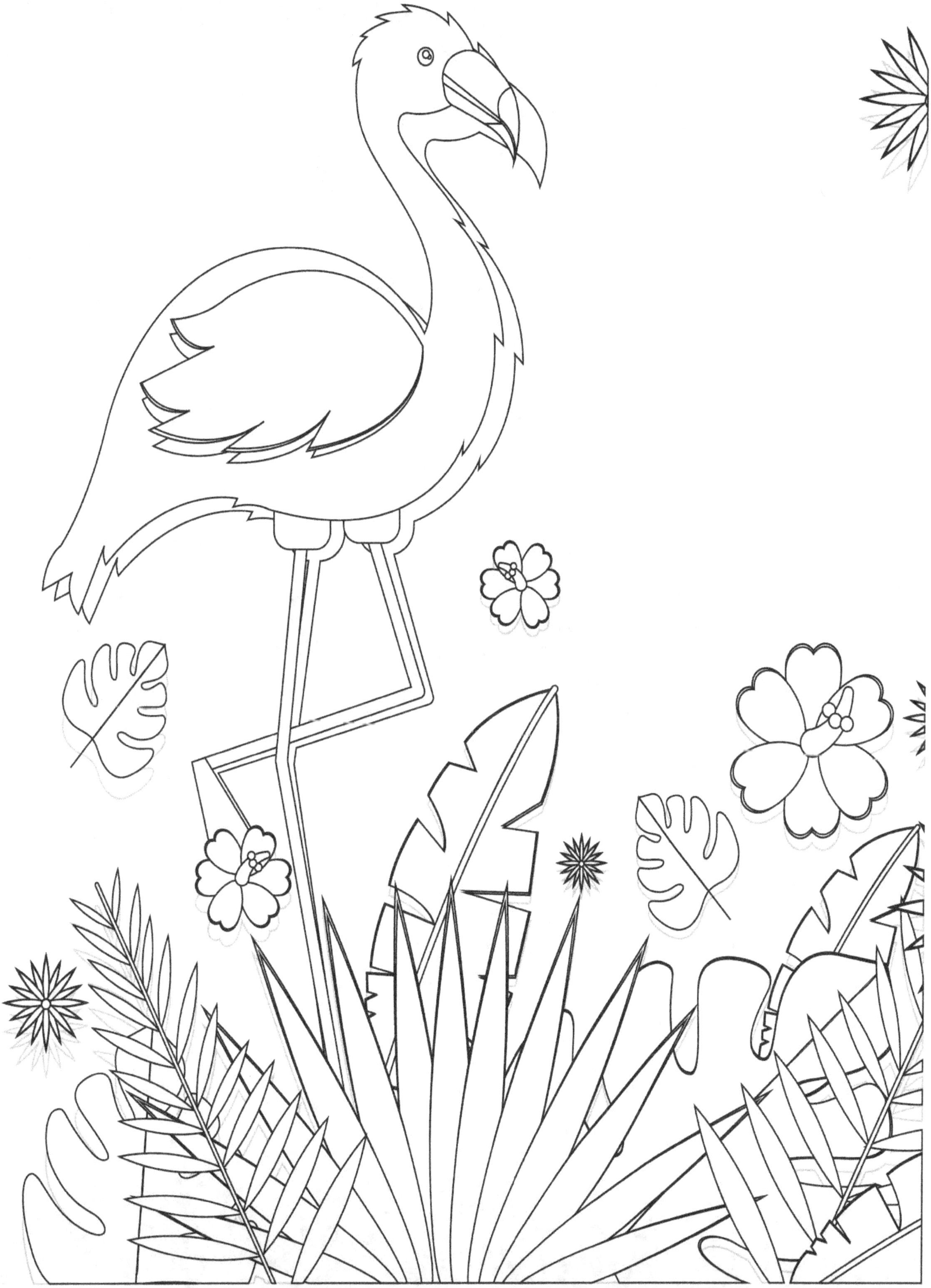

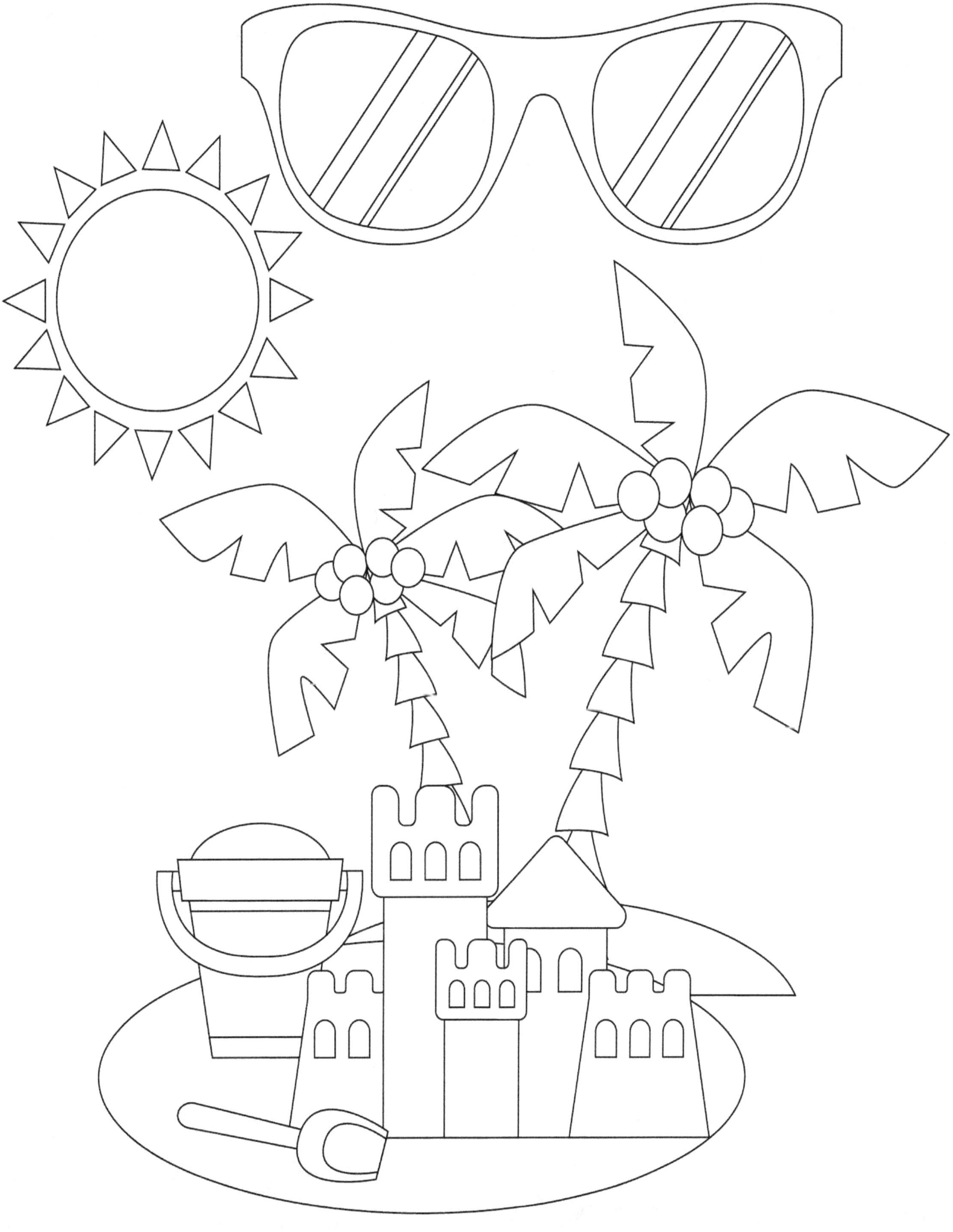

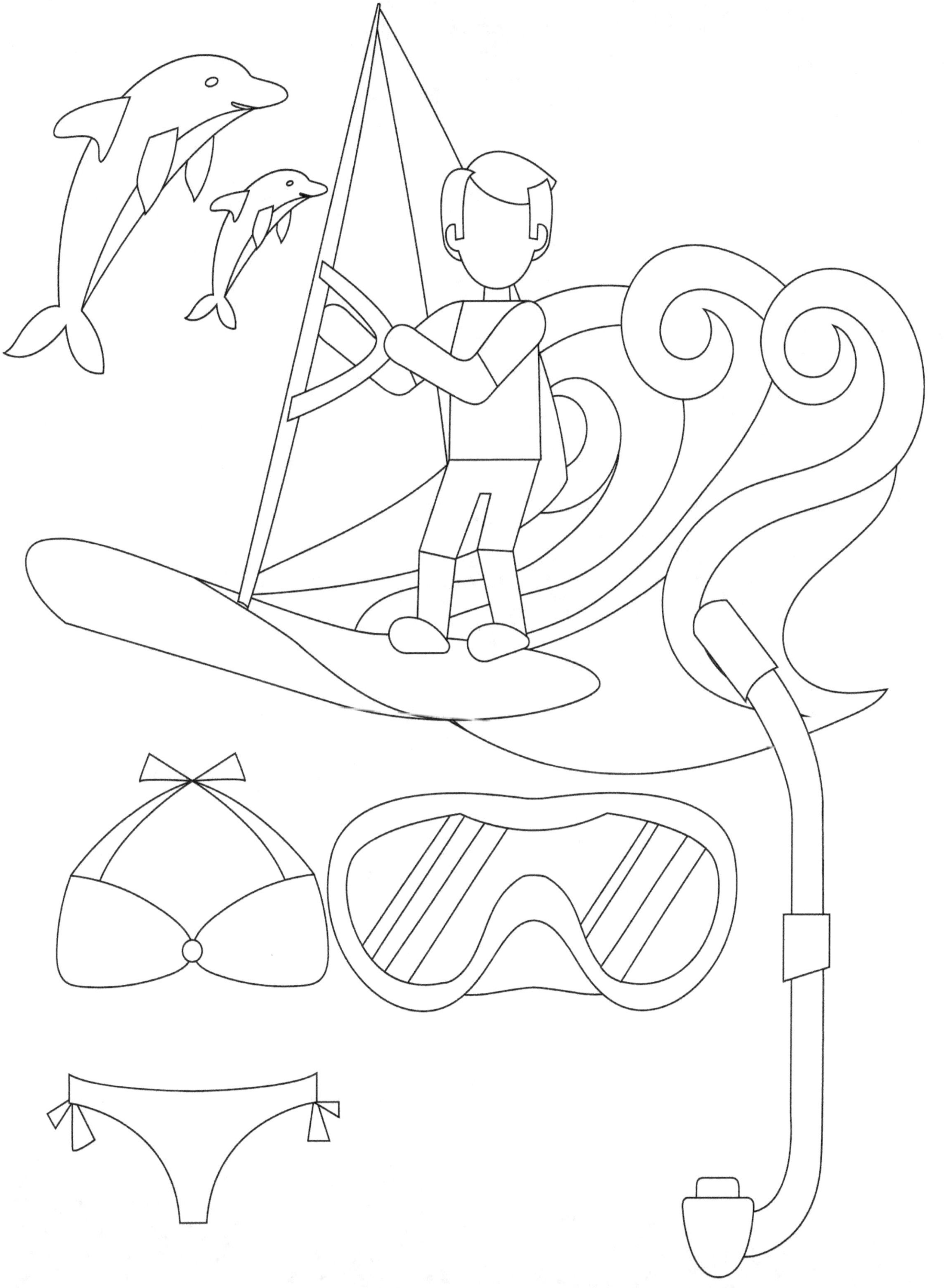

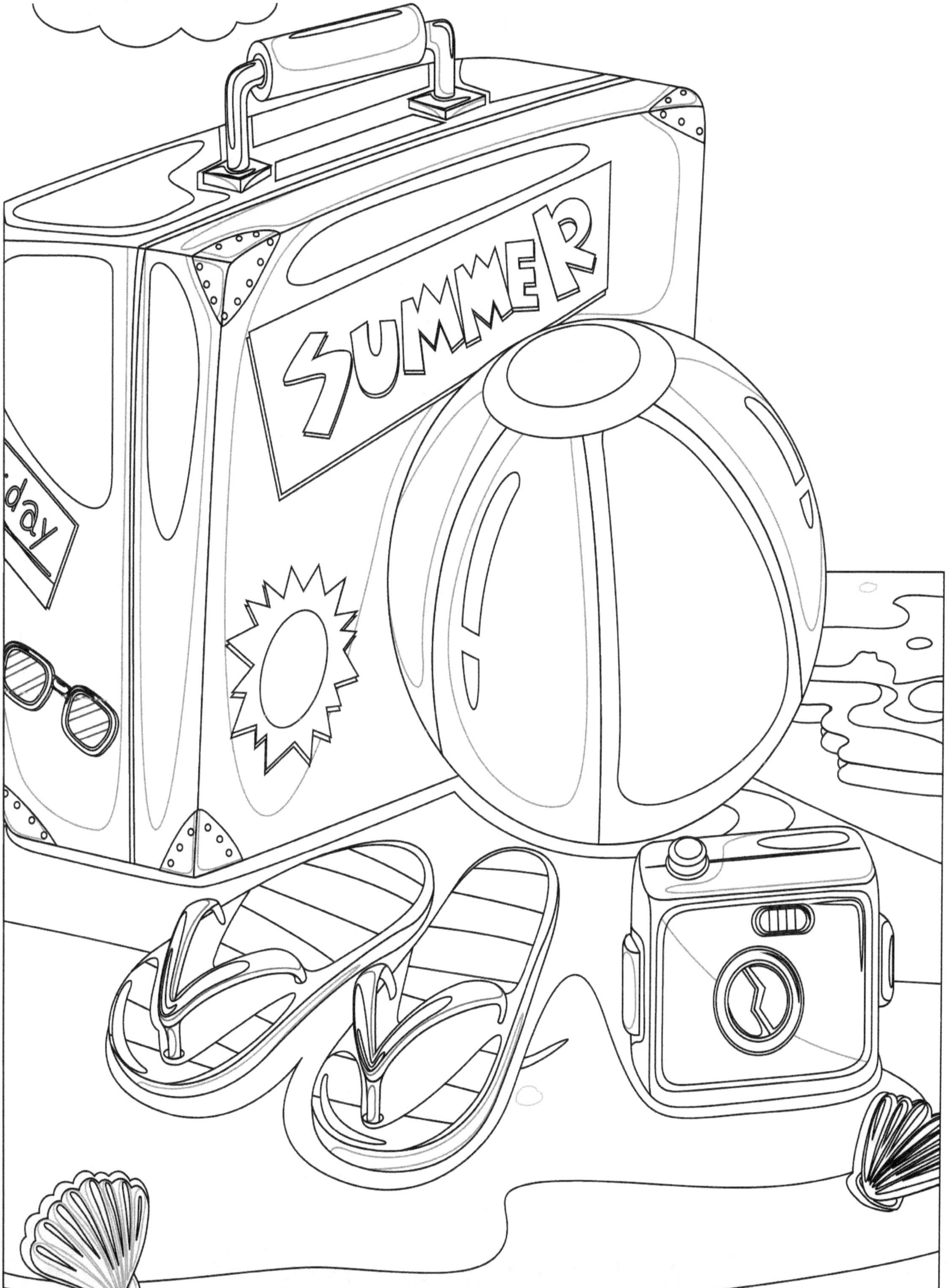
SUMMER
day

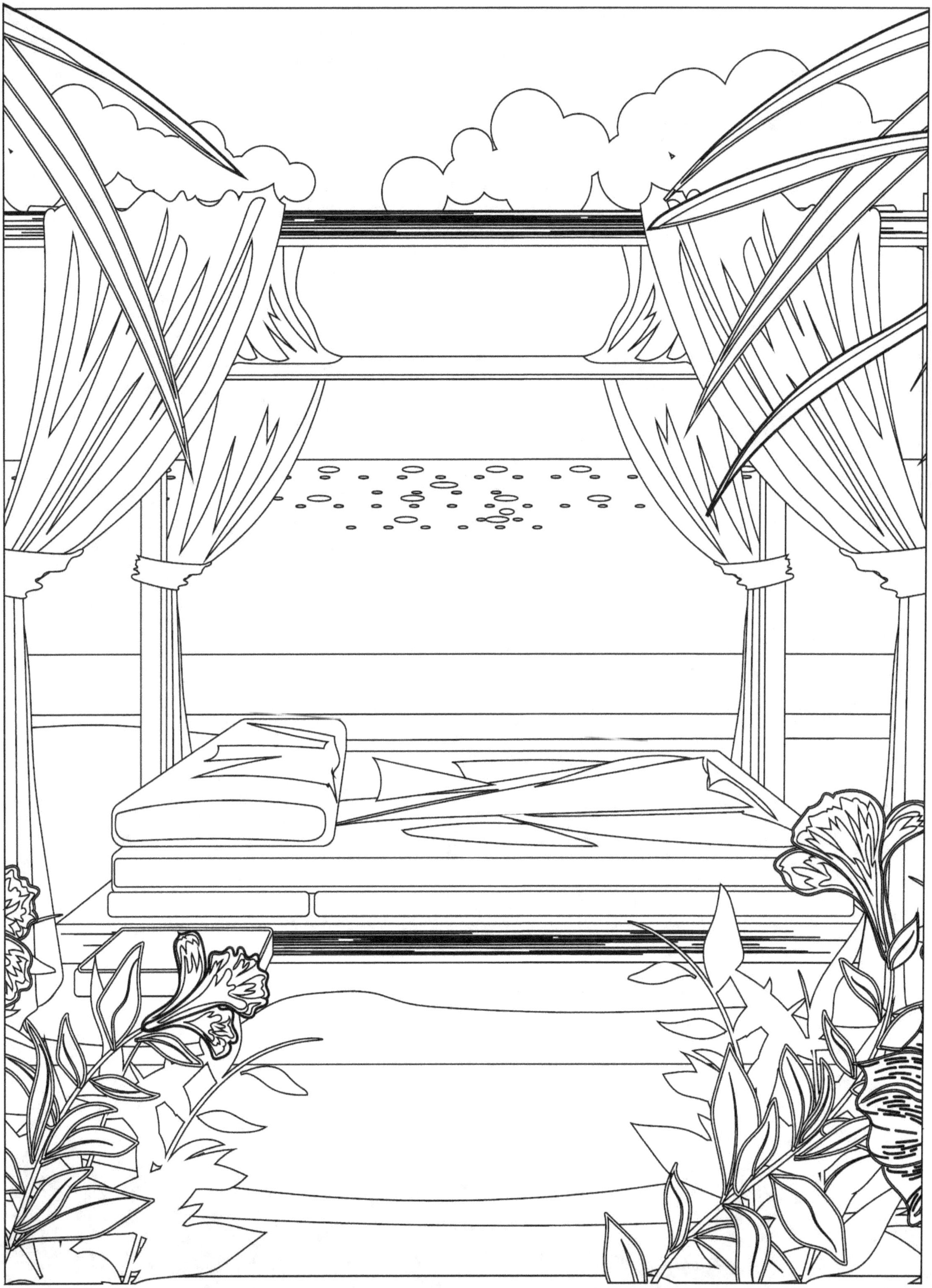

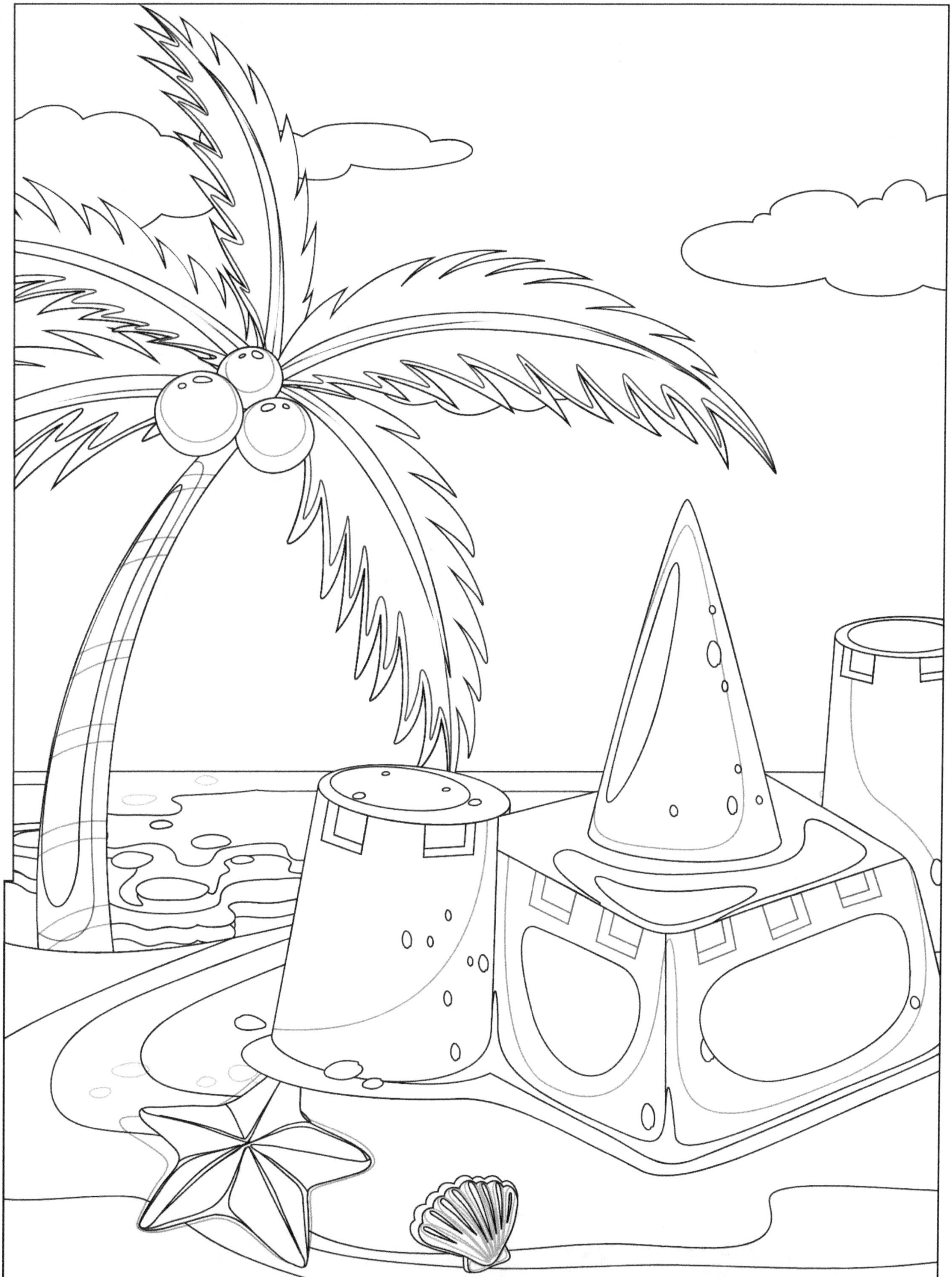

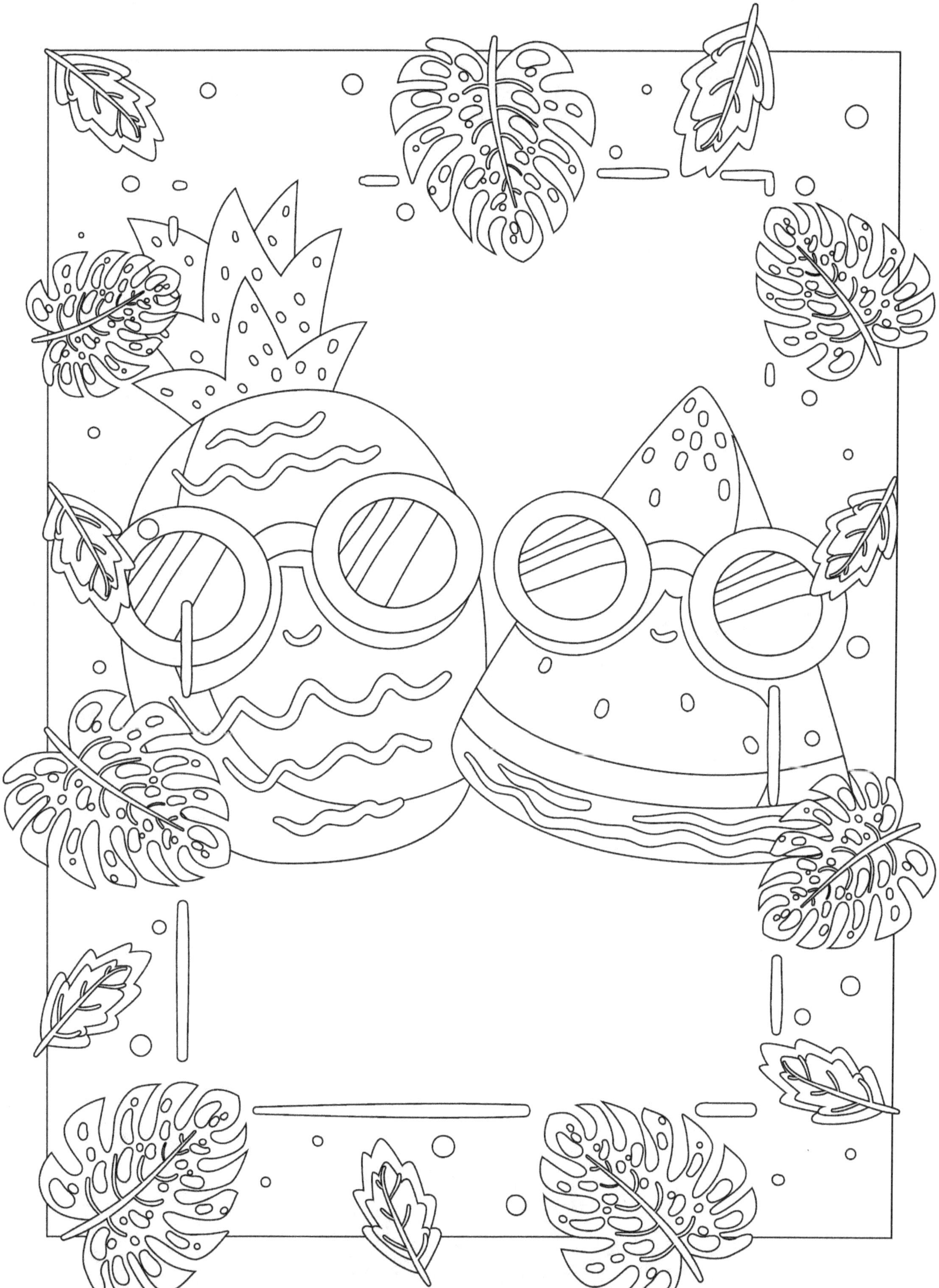

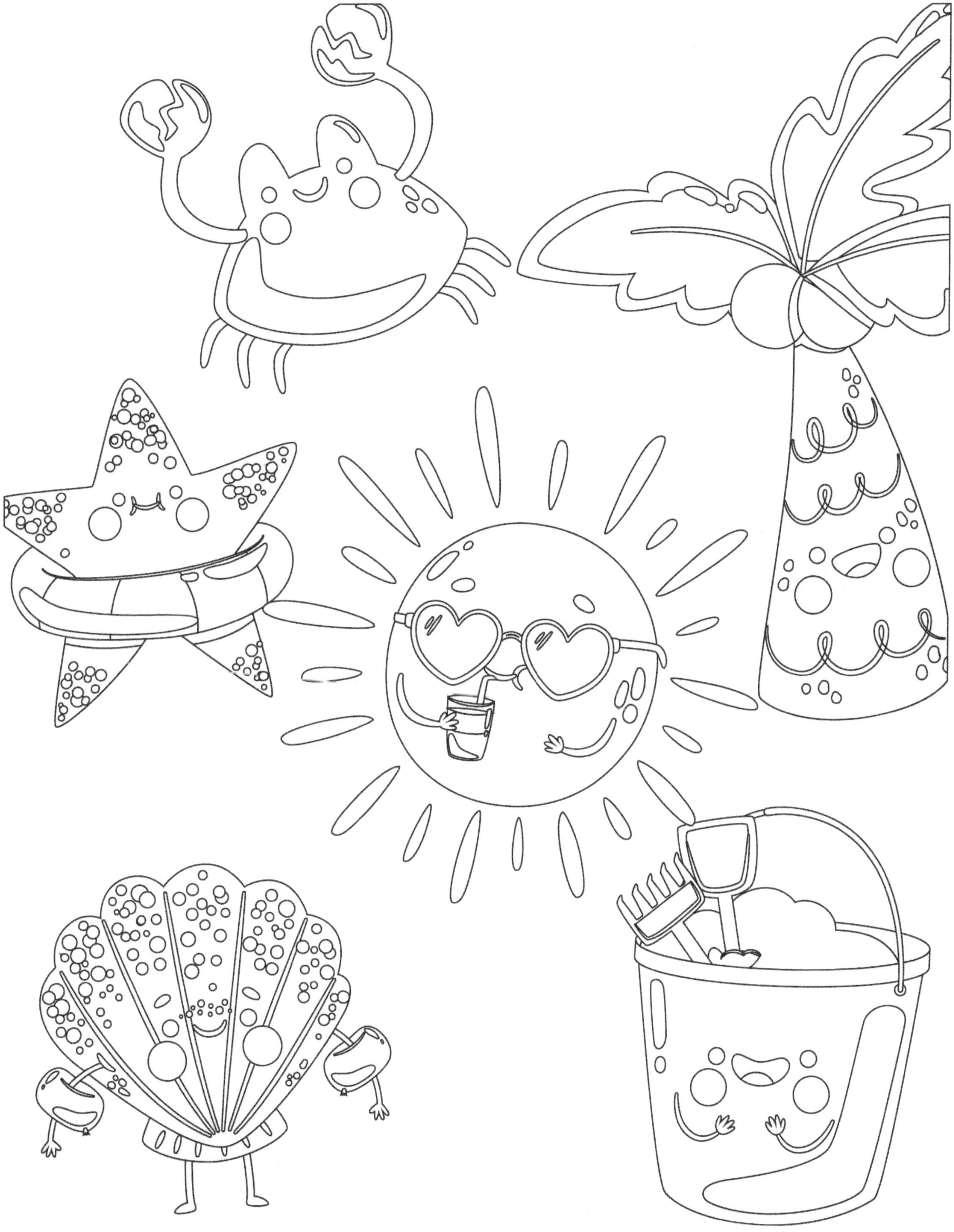

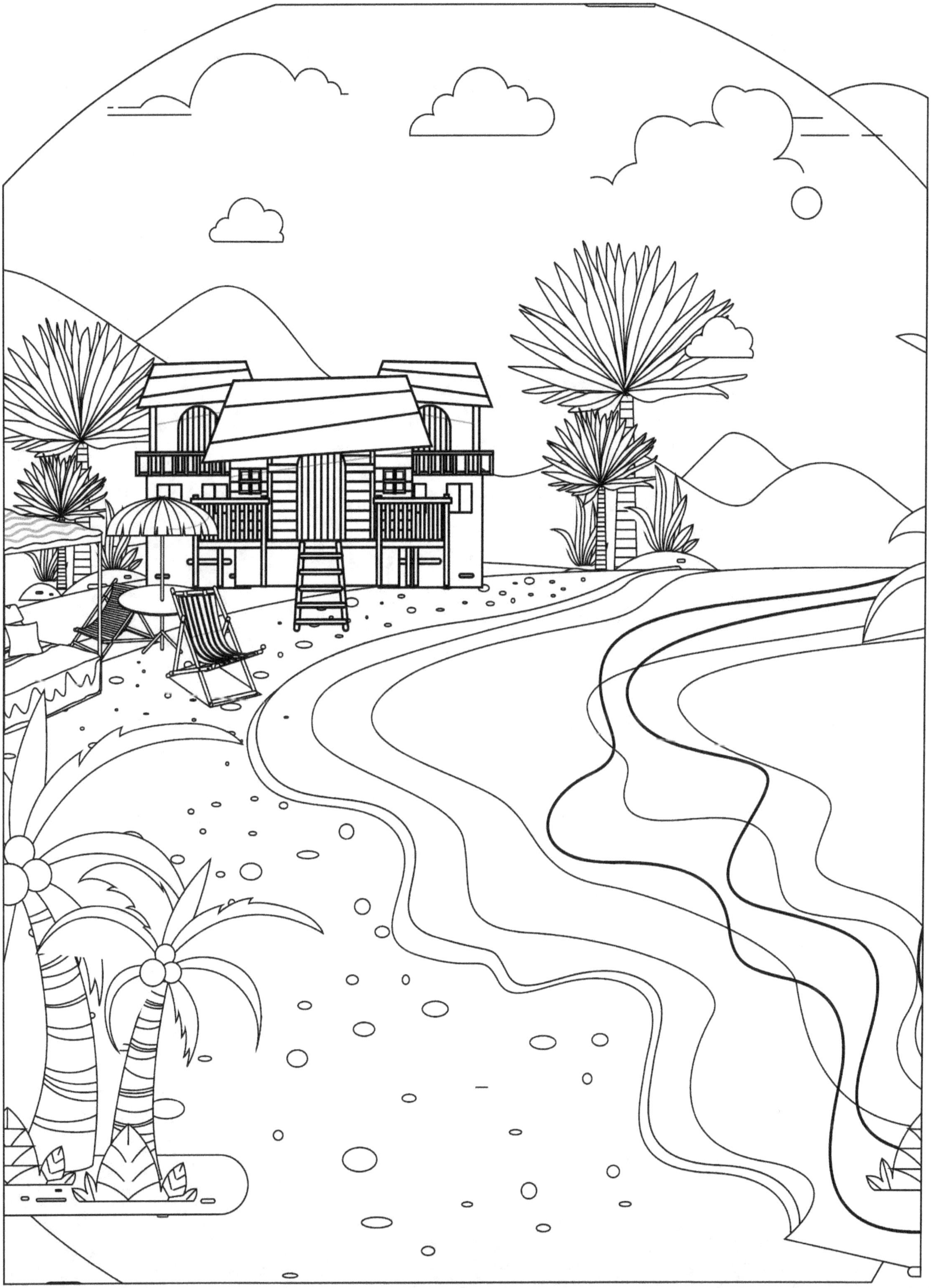

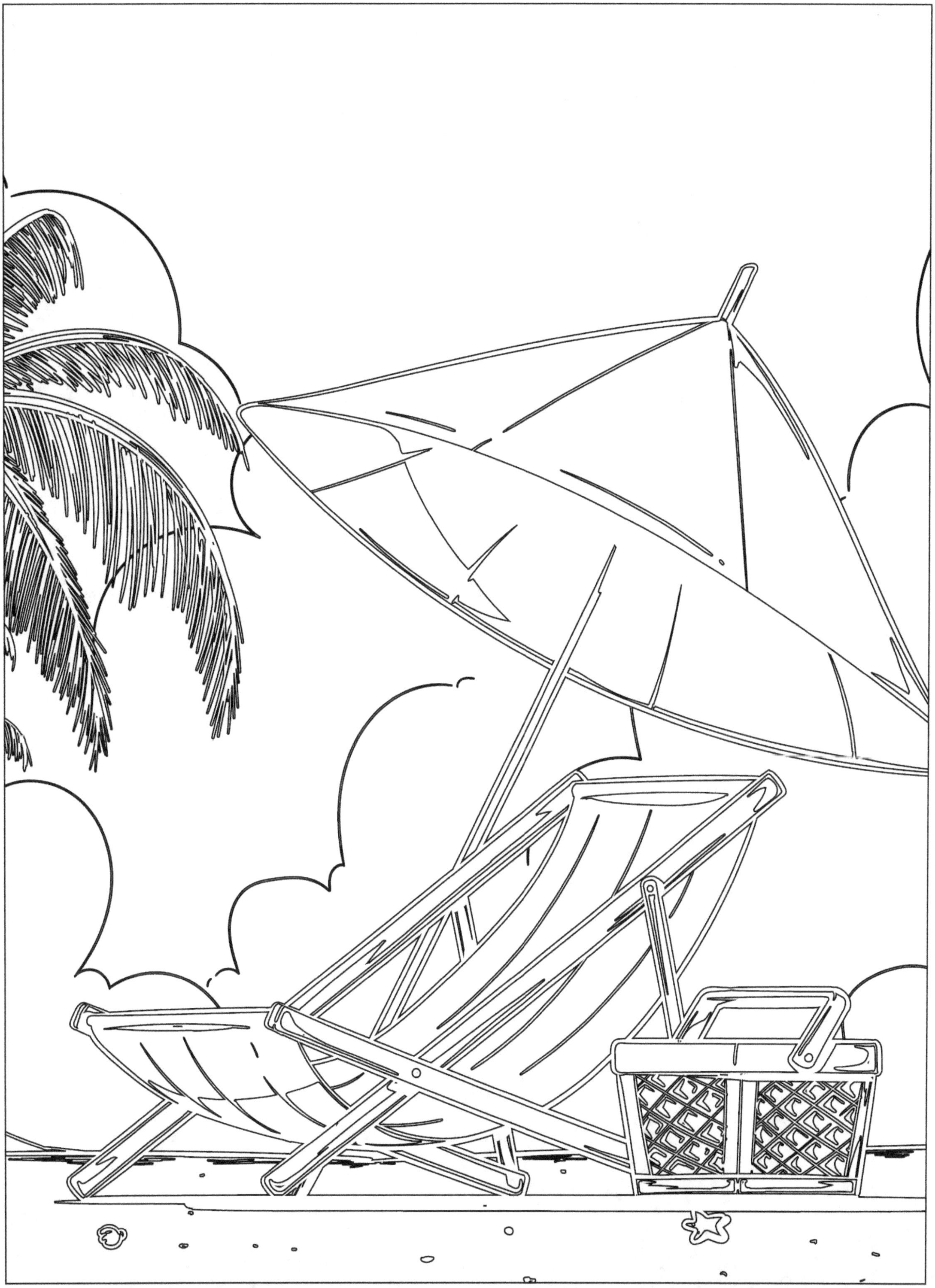

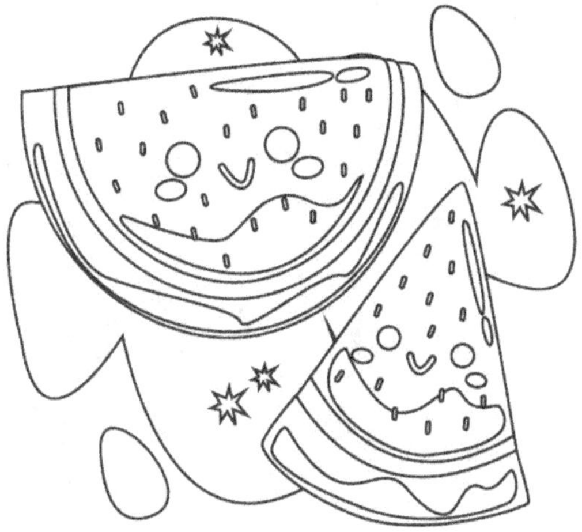
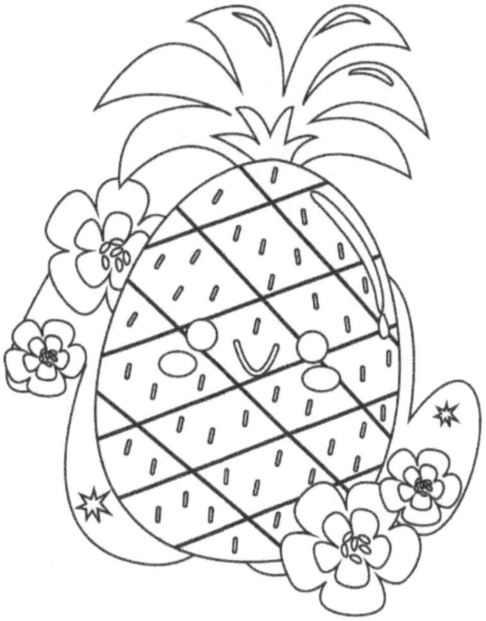
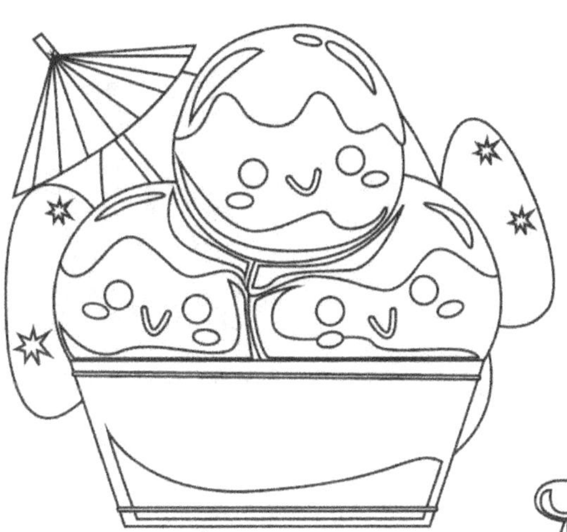
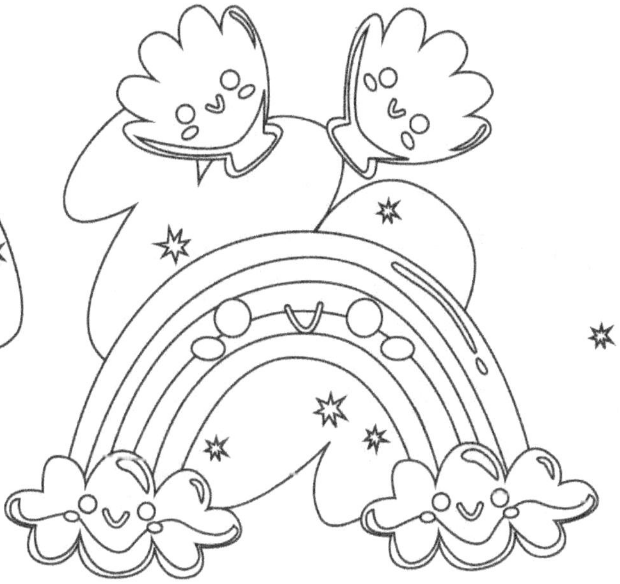
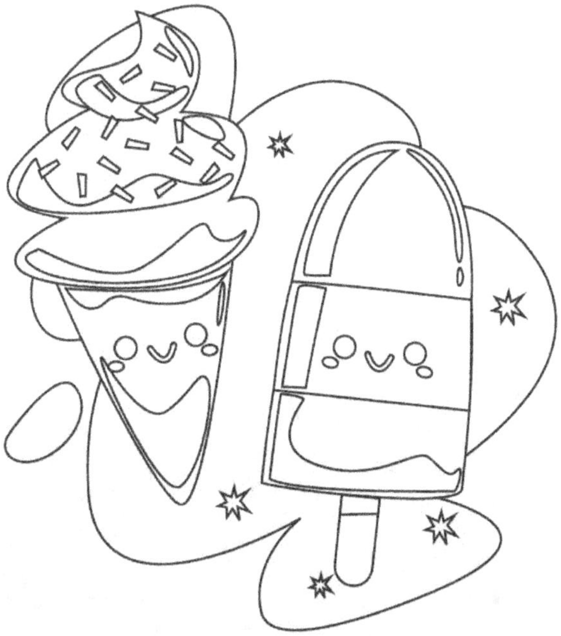
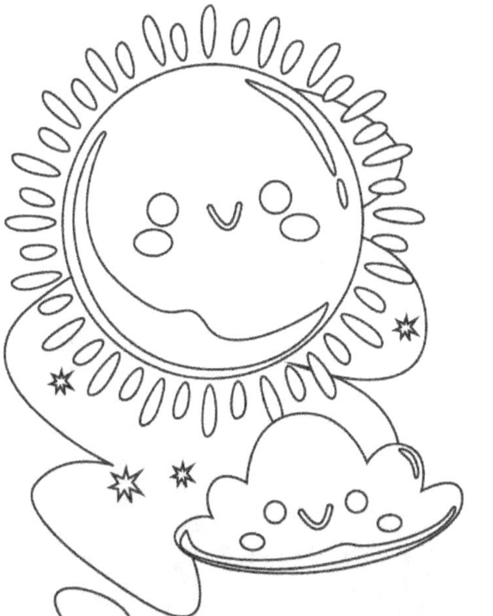

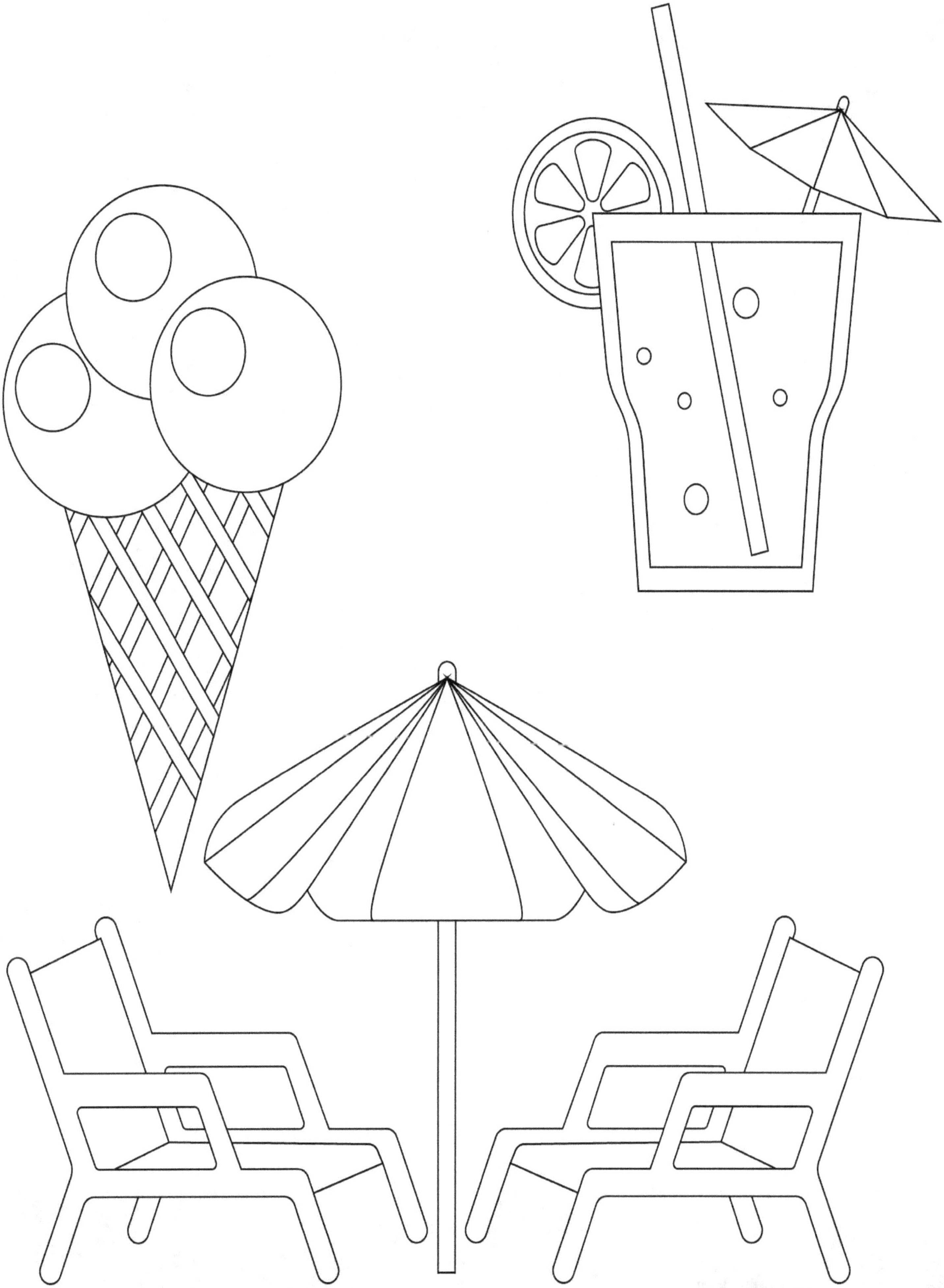

www.ingramcontent.com/pod-product-compliance
Lightning Source LLC
Chambersburg PA
CBHW080853220526
45467CB00008B/2497
* 9 7 9 8 7 2 9 0 4 5 6 7 9 *